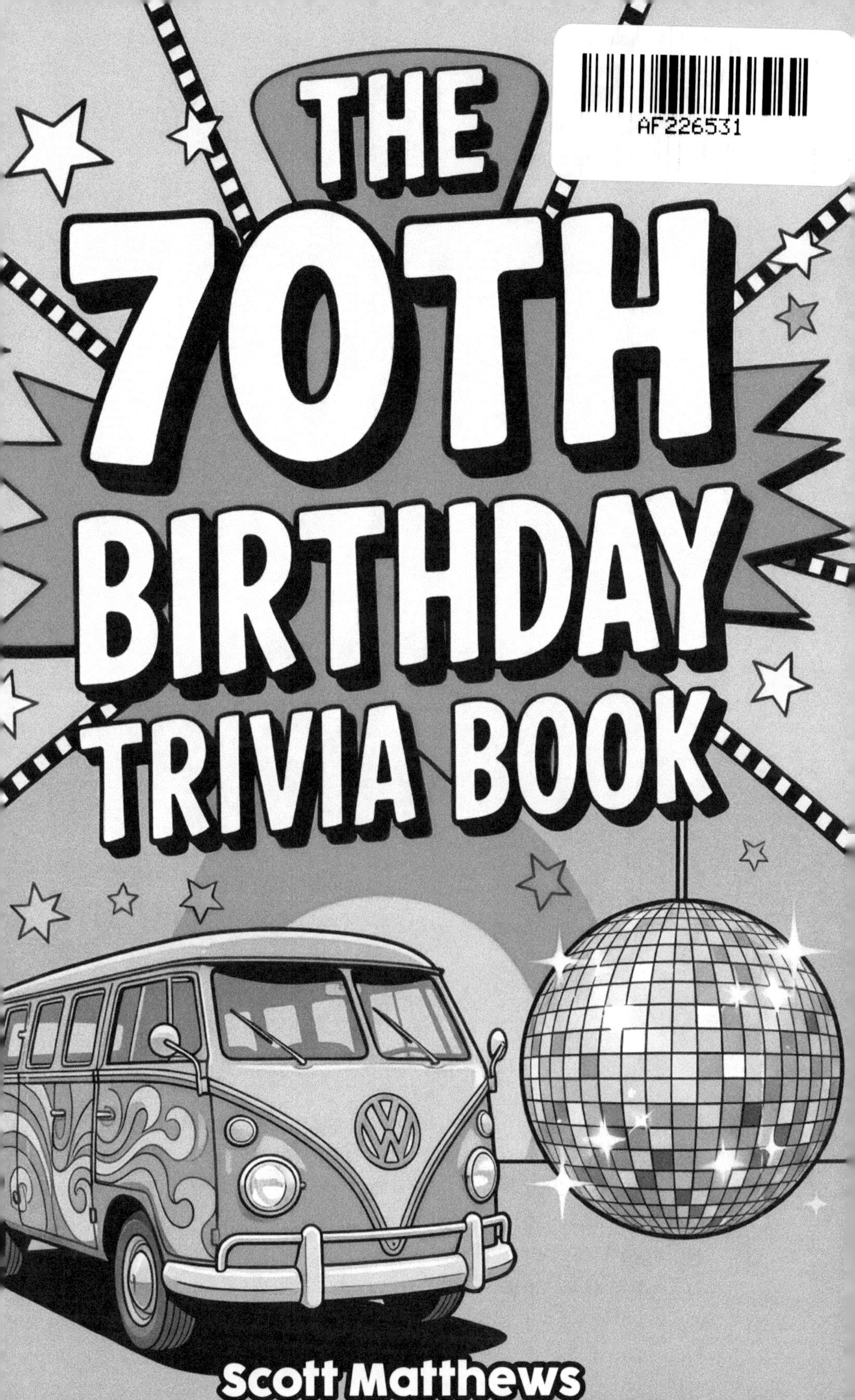

AF226531
THE
70TH
BIRTHDAY
TRIVIA BOOK
Scott Matthews

CONTENT

INTRODUCTION

Seventy years. Seven full decades of change, challenge, music, laughter, and moments that shaped not just the world, but your world.

You were born into a time of rabbit-ear TVs, phones on the wall, handwritten letters, and milk delivered in glass bottles. If someone wanted to reach you, they had to call the house and hope you were home. If you missed your favorite show, you truly missed it. Life moved a little slower, but somehow felt just as full.

Since then, you've watched the world transform in ways no generation before you ever experienced. You saw rock and roll explode, watched man walk on the moon, lived through the Cold War, disco, and the birth of the internet. You witnessed smartphones take over daily life and streaming replace everything that once came on a schedule. Vinyl turned into cassettes, then CDs, then playlists in your pocket.

You grew up outdoors, memorized phone numbers, and navigated without GPS. You learned patience in a world that didn't move at lightning speed. And yet here you are, not just keeping up, but thriving in one of the most advanced eras in human history.

Turning 70 isn't just about age. It's about perspective. It's about having a front-row seat to history. It's about remembering when gas was cheap, when Saturday morning cartoons were sacred, and when a single song could define an entire summer.

This book is a celebration of that journey. Inside, you'll revisit the decades that shaped you, from childhood memories to cultural shifts and unforgettable moments. You'll test your memory, laugh at long-forgotten fads, and debate events that somehow feel like yesterday.

Some questions will make you smile. Some will surprise you. A few might have you saying, "No way that was that long ago."

This isn't just a trivia book. It's a time machine. A game-night companion. A conversation starter. And if you choose to fill in the memory pages, it becomes something even more meaningful, a snapshot of your own story.

So gather the family, split into teams, keep score, and don't be afraid to argue a little along the way. Laugh often, share stories, and enjoy the memories that come rushing back.

And as you turn the page, remember this: You didn't just live through history, you are part of it.

Welcome to 70!

Childhood Days: The 50s & Early 60s

Life in the late 1950s and early 1960s moved at a slower, steadier pace, shaped by simple routines and familiar traditions. Kids rode their bikes until dark, families gathered around a single television set, and the radio played in kitchens and cars. Phones had cords, milk came in glass bottles, and Saturday mornings felt special. It was a time of jukebox hits, drive-in theaters, chrome-trimmed cars, and advertising slogans everyone seemed to know by heart. Neighborhoods felt close, prices were modest, and entertainment did not depend on passwords or charging cables. Those everyday details may seem small now, but they built the foundation of a generation's memories. Let's revisit the sights, sounds, and habits that defined childhood during those early years.

1. In many American classrooms during the early 1960s, which of the following items was commonly found hanging near the chalkboard?

a. A world map with updated country borders
b. A portrait of the current President
c. A large film projector screen
d. A television mounted in the corner

2. Which of the following products was famously advertised with the slogan "Plop, plop, fizz, fizz"?

a. Alka-Seltzer
b. Coca-Cola
c. Pepto-Bismol
d. 7-Up

3. In 1963, which toy became an instant craze after being demonstrated on The Tonight Show?

a. Etch A Sketch
b. Easy-Bake Oven
c. Hula Hoop
d. Chatty Cathy

4. What was the standard speed for most 45 rpm vinyl singles that teenagers played on record players in the 1960s?

a. 33 1/3 rpm
b. 45 rpm
c. 78 rpm
d. 16 rpm

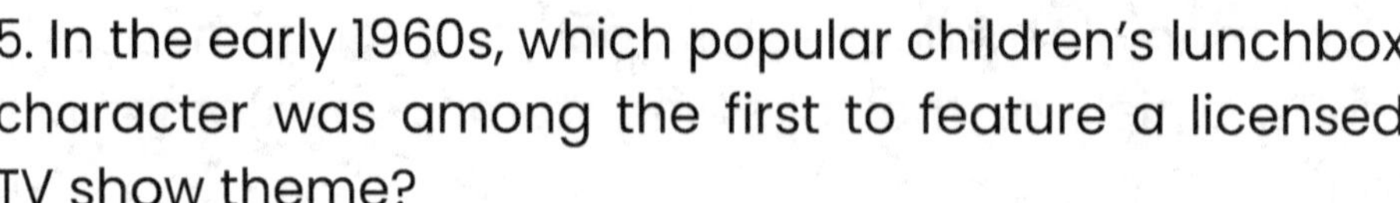

5. In the early 1960s, which popular children's lunchbox character was among the first to feature a licensed TV show theme?

a. The Flintstones
b. Hopalong Cassidy
c. Batman
d. Scooby-Doo

6. Around 1960, approximately how much did a gallon of gasoline cost in the United States?

a. About $1.25
b. About $0.75
c. About $0.31
d. About $0.10

7. Which of these items would most likely have been found in a classroom during the late 1950s?

a. An overhead transparency projector
b. An inkwell built into the desk
c. A digital clock
d. A photocopier

8. The phrase "Be seeing you" became widely recognized from which 1960s television series?

a. The Twilight Zone
b. Gilligan's Island
c. The Prisoner
d. Bonanza

9. Which board game, originally released in the 1930s but massively popular in 1950s households?

a. Risk
b. Clue
c. Monopoly
d. Life

10. In the 1960s, what was commonly used to dry freshly washed laundry in many suburban backyards?

a. Electric dryer only
b. Clothesline strung between poles
c. Portable heater rack
d. Indoor drying cabinet

11. In the early 1960s, which popular household appliance was still considered a luxury in many homes?

a. Refrigerator
b. Electric stove
c. Color television
d. Vacuum cleaner

12. Which brand used the famous advertising slogan "Snap, Crackle, Pop" during the 1950s and 60s?

a. Corn Flakes
b. Cheerios
c. Rice Krispies
d. Wheaties

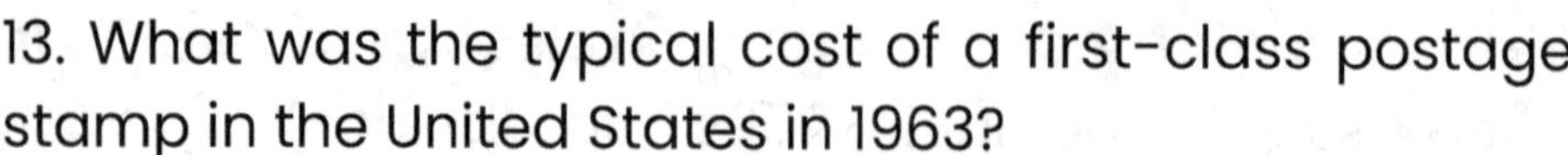

13. What was the typical cost of a first-class postage stamp in the United States in 1963?

a. 2 cents
b. 4 cents
c. 5 cents
d. 10 cents

14. Which toy, consisting of two wooden paddles connected by a rubber ball on an elastic string, was popular with children in the 1960s?

a. Skip-It
b. Paddle Ball
c. Yo-Yo Pro
d. Toss Catch

15. Which fast-food chain, founded in the 1940s, began rapidly expanding across America during the 1950s and 60s?

a. Burger King
b. Wendy's
c. Taco Bell
d. McDonald's

16. Which popular board game, first released in 1960, featured a plastic bubble in the middle that players pressed to roll the dice?

a. Trouble
b. Operation

c. The Game of Life
d. Sorry

17. In many homes during the late 1950s, where was the primary household telephone most commonly installed?

a. On a small table in the front hallway
b. Mounted on the kitchen wall near the doorway
c. On a bedside nightstand in the master bedroom
d. Inside a built-in cabinet in the living room

18. Which children's TV program that premiered in 1955 featured a clubhouse and a group of mouse-eared hosts?

a. Captain Kangaroo
b. Romper Room
c. The Mickey Mouse Club
d. Howdy Doody

19. What was commonly used in classrooms before ballpoint pens became widespread?

a. Felt-tip markers
b. Fountain pens
c. Mechanical pencils
d. Gel pens

20. In the early 1960s, approximately how much did the average new car cost in the United States?
a. Around $1,200

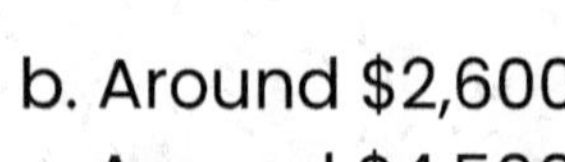

b. Around $2,600
c. Around $4,500
d. Around $7,000

CHAPTER 1 ANSWERS

1. b) A portrait of the current President - Many classrooms displayed a framed photo of the sitting President near the chalkboard as a symbol of civic pride and national identity.

2. a) Alka-Seltzer - The catchy "Plop, plop, fizz, fizz" jingle became one of the most memorable advertising slogans of the era.

3. a) Etch A Sketch - Demonstrated on national television, it quickly became a must-have toy for children fascinated by its magical disappearing drawings.

4. b) 45 rpm - Most hit singles were pressed on 45 rpm records, making them the soundtrack of teenage bedrooms and sock hops.

5. b) Hopalong Cassidy - Hopalong Cassidy was one of the earliest television characters to be heavily licensed for merchandise, including metal lunchboxes that became playground status symbols in the 1950s and early 1960s.

6. c) About $0.31 - Gasoline around 1960 averaged just over thirty cents per gallon, a price that feels almost unreal today.

7. b) An inkwell built into the desk - Many older school desks still had built-in inkwell holes, even after fountain pens began replacing dip pens.

8. c) *The Prisoner* - The British series *The Prisoner* made the line "Be seeing you" a memorable cultural catchphrase.

9. c) Monopoly - Though introduced in the 1930s, Monopoly became a staple of family game nights throughout the 1950s.

10. b) Clothesline strung between poles - Backyard clotheslines were common in suburban neighborhoods before dryers became universal.

11. c) Color television - While black-and-white sets were widespread, color TVs were still considered a luxury purchase in the early 1960s.

12. c) Rice Krispies - The "Snap, Crackle, Pop" slogan became one of the most recognizable cereal advertisements of the era.

13. c) 5 cents - In 1963, a first-class postage stamp cost just five cents.

14. b) Paddle Ball - The wooden paddle with a rubber ball attached by elastic provided simple but addictive backyard entertainment.

15. d) McDonald's - The chain expanded rapidly in the 1950s and 60s, helping shape modern fast-food culture.

16. a) Trouble - The plastic bubble used to "pop" the dice became the signature feature of the board game Trouble.

17. b) Mounted on the kitchen wall near the doorway - The kitchen was often the central hub of the home, making it the most practical location for the main telephone.

18. c) The Mickey Mouse Club - Premiering in 1955, it featured a clubhouse setting and young hosts wearing mouse ears.

19. b) Fountain pens - Before ballpoints became standard, fountain pens were widely used in classrooms and required refilling.

20. b) Around $2,600 - The average new car in the early 1960s cost roughly twenty-six hundred dollars.

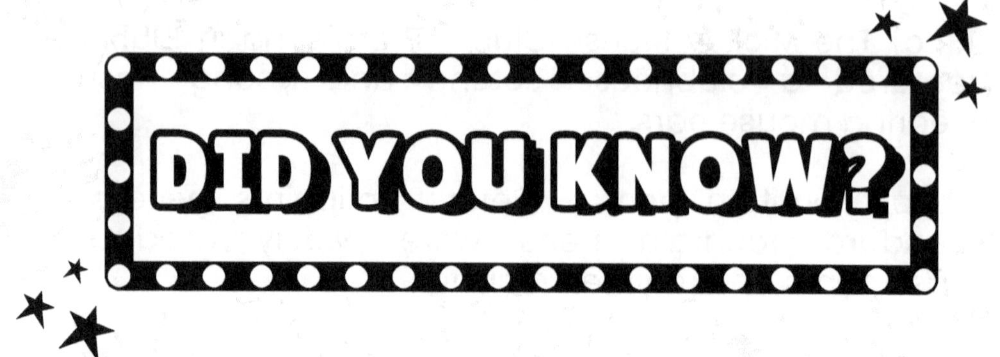

When Mr. Potato Head hit store shelves in 1952, it made history as the very first toy to be advertised on television. The original version didn't even include a plastic potato body; instead, parents had to provide a real potato or other vegetable for their children to poke the plastic facial features into. The commercials were revolutionary because they were aimed directly at children rather than their parents, changing how toys were marketed forever.

The iconic Hula Hoop sparked one of the most intense, short-lived fads in American history during the late 1950s. After Wham-O introduced the plastic hoops in 1958, they sold an astonishing 25 million units in just the first four months. While the craze died down almost as quickly as it started, the Hula Hoop cemented its place in pop culture and was officially patented in 1963.

The early days of television news were incredibly different from today's 24-hour cycle. In 1952, the *TODAY* show premiered as one of the first morning news and entertainment programs. That same year marked the first time television networks were able to broadcast the Republican and Democratic national conventions live, bringing the excitement of national politics directly into American living rooms for the very first time.

Finding Your Voice: The Teenage 60s

The 1960s were bold, restless, and unforgettable. For many, these were the years of first cars, first concerts, first dances, and real independence. Music wasn't just background noise, it became part of who you were, with bands debated, lyrics memorized, and one hit song able to define a summer. Television grew, fashion changed quickly, and teenagers began shaping culture instead of following it. Headlines were powerful, filled with protests, speeches, and space missions that captured the world's attention. Yet beyond those big moments, daily life was simple, built around friends, cruising in cars, saving for records, and dreaming about the future. The 1960s shaped a generation in ways that still feel vivid today.

1. Which British band sparked what became known as the "British Invasion" in the United States in 1964?

a. The Rolling Stones
b. The Who
c. The Beatles
d. The Kinks

2. Which dance craze became wildly popular among teenagers in the early 1960s after a hit song by Chubby Checker?

a. The Twist
b. The Mashed Potato
c. The Pony
d. The Watusi

3. In the 1960s, what was a common way for teenagers to listen to their favorite music privately?

a. Portable cassette player
b. Transistor radio
c. 8-track player
d. CD player

4. Which popular 1969 music festival became a defining moment of the counterculture movement?

a. Monterey Pop Festival
b. Altamont Free Concert
c. Woodstock
d. Lollapalooza

5. Which car was introduced in 1964 and quickly became a symbol of teenage freedom and muscle car culture?

a. Chevrolet Camaro
b. Ford Mustang
c. Pontiac GTO
d. Dodge Charger

6. In 1967, which Beatles album featured the songs "Lucy in the Sky with Diamonds" and "A Day in the Life"?

a. Rubber Soul
b. Revolver
c. Sgt. Pepper's Lonely Hearts Club Band
d. Abbey Road

7. What item did many teenage girls in the 1960s use to straighten their hair before modern flat irons existed?

a. Curling iron
b. Heated rollers
c. Clothes iron
d. Hair dryer

8. In December 1969, what method was used to determine the draft order for 19-year-old men in the United States?

a. Alphabetical order by last name
b. College enrollment status

c. Birthdate lottery drawing
d. Random selection by Social Security number

9. Which snack food, introduced in the 1960s, became famous for its slogan "Once you pop, you can't stop"?

a. Doritos
b. Cheetos
c. Lay's
d. Pringles

10. Which fashion trend became popular among teenage boys in the late 1960s, often worn with patterned shirts and longer hair?

a. Crew cuts and letterman jackets
b. Three-piece suits
c. Bell-bottom jeans
d. Leather biker jackets

11. In 1969, which Supreme Court case ruled that public school students do not "shed their constitutional rights to freedom of speech or expression at the schoolhouse gate"?

a. Brown v. Board of Education
b. Miranda v. Arizona
c. Tinker v. Des Moines
d. Roe v. Wade

12. Which 1966 Beach Boys album is widely considered one of the most influential pop albums ever recorded?

a. Surfin' USA
b. Pet Sounds
c. Endless Summer
d. Little Deuce Coupe

13. In 1964, which boxer defeated Sonny Liston to become the youngest heavyweight champion in history at the time?

a. Joe Frazier
b. George Foreman
c. Muhammad Ali
d. Floyd Patterson

14. Which 1967 film, starring Dustin Hoffman, featured the famous line, "Mrs. Robinson, you're trying to seduce me"?

a. Bonnie and Clyde
b. Easy Rider
c. Guess Who's Coming to Dinner
d. The Graduate

15. In 1963, which civil rights leader delivered the "I Have a Dream" speech during the March on Washington?

a. Malcolm X
b. Thurgood Marshall
c. Jesse Jackson
d. Martin Luther King Jr.

16. In 1968, which athlete raised a black-gloved fist on a the medal podium at the Mexico City Olympics?

a. Tommie Smith
b. Jim Brown
c. Wilt Chamberlain
d. Carl Lewis

17. During the Apollo 11 mission in July 1969, which astronaut remained inside the command module while Neil Armstrong and Buzz Aldrin walked on the moon?

a. Michael Collins
b. Alan Shepard
c. Jim Lovell
d. John Glenn

18. In 1967, which U.S. state became the first to lower the voting age to 18 for state and local elections?

a. California
b. Texas
c. Georgia
d. New York

19. Which 1966 television series featured a spaceship called the USS Enterprise?

a. Lost in Space
b. The Outer Limits
c. Battlestar Galactica
d. Star Trek

20. In 1962, which artist recorded the hit song "Blowin' in the Wind," which became associated with the civil rights movement?

a. Joan Baez
b. Peter, Paul and Mary
c. Johnny Cash
d. Bob Dylan

CHAPTER 2 ANSWERS

1. c) The Beatles – Their 1964 appearance on The Ed Sullivan Show launched the British Invasion and changed American pop culture overnight.

2. a) The Twist – Chubby Checker's hit made the dance a nationwide sensation and a staple at teen parties.

3. b) Transistor radio – Small, portable, and battery-powered, it let teenagers listen to music privately for the first time.

4. c) Woodstock – Held in August 1969, it became the defining music festival of the counterculture era.

5. b) Ford Mustang – Introduced in 1964, it quickly became an affordable performance car that symbolized teenage freedom.

6. c) Sgt. Pepper's Lonely Hearts Club Band – Released in 1967, it featured both "Lucy in the Sky with Diamonds" and "A Day in the Life."

7. c) Clothes iron – Before modern flat irons, some girls literally used a household clothes iron to straighten their hair.

8. c) Birthdate lottery drawing – In December 1969, birth dates were randomly drawn to determine draft order for the Vietnam War.

9. d) Pringles - The slogan "Once you pop, you can't stop" became one of the most memorable snack ads of the era.

10. c) Bell-bottom jeans - Popular in the late 1960s, they became closely associated with youth culture and the counterculture movement.

11. c) Tinker v. Des Moines - The 1965 case affirmed that students retain certain constitutional rights in public schools.

12. b) Pet Sounds - The 1966 album is widely regarded as one of the most influential recordings in pop music history.

13. c) Muhammad Ali - In 1964, he defeated Sonny Liston to become the youngest heavyweight champion at the time.

14. d) The Graduate - The 1967 film became iconic for its portrayal of youth uncertainty and social change.

15. d) Martin Luther King Jr. - He delivered the "I Have a Dream" speech during the 1963 March on Washington.

16. a) Tommie Smith - He raised his black-gloved fist during the medal ceremony at the 1968 Mexico City Olympics.

17. a) Michael Collins - He remained in the command module orbiting the moon while Armstrong and Aldrin walked on the surface.

18. c) Georgia - In 1967, Georgia lowered the voting age to 18 for state and local elections before it became national law.

19. d) Star Trek - Premiering in 1966, it featured the starship USS Enterprise.

20. d) Bob Dylan - He recorded "Blowin' in the Wind" in 1962, and it became closely associated with the civil rights movement.

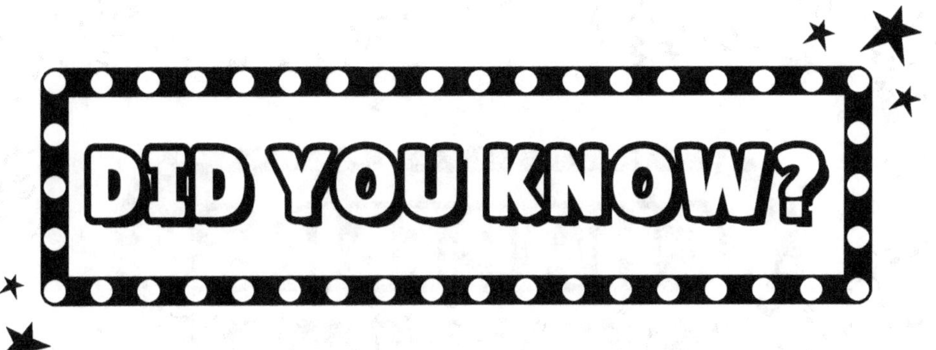

The very first Super Bowl, played on January 15, 1967, between the Green Bay Packers and the Kansas City Chiefs, wasn't even called the "Super Bowl" at the time. It was officially known as the "AFL-NFL World Championship Game." It remains the only Super Bowl in history to be broadcast simultaneously on two different television networks (CBS and NBC), as each network held the rights to one of the competing leagues.

During the height of the Space Race, the Apollo 11 mission almost didn't include the famous phrase "That's one small step for man, one giant leap for mankind." Neil Armstrong claimed he actually said "for a man," but the "a" was lost in transmission static.

The 1960s saw the birth of pop art, fundamentally changing how the world viewed everyday objects. Artists like Andy Warhol turned ordinary items like Campbell's Soup cans and Coca-Cola bottles into high-priced gallery exhibits. This movement challenged traditional art by embracing commercialism and mass production, perfectly reflecting the rapidly growing consumer culture of the decade.

The Disco & Revolution Years: The 70s

The 1970s were bold, loud, and impossible to ignore. It was a decade of disco lights, blockbuster movies, political drama, and unforgettable music that filled dance floors and car radios alike. Gas lines stretched around corners while arcades buzzed with early video games. Fashion made statements with platform shoes, bell bottoms, and wide collars, and television became even more central to everyday life. From championship victories to cultural shifts that reshaped society, the 70s carried both tension and celebration, becoming a decade defined by strong personalities, powerful headlines, and moments that still feel unforgettable today.

1. In 1977, which film became the highest-grossing movie of its time and launched a massive sci-fi franchise?

a. Close Encounters of the Third Kind
b. Star Wars
c. The Godfather
d. Jaws

2. Which music group dominated the disco era with hits like "Stayin' Alive" and "Night Fever"?

a. ABBA
b. The Rolling Stones
c. Bee Gees
d. Earth, Wind and Fire

3. In 1973, which major political scandal led to the resignation of President Richard Nixon?

a. The Pentagon Papers
b. The Iran Hostage Crisis
c. The Oil Embargo
d. Watergate

4. Which arcade game, released in 1978, became one of the first major video game crazes?

a. Asteroids
b. Donkey Kong
c. Galaga
d. Space Invaders

5. Which footwear trend became wildly popular in the 1970s, often worn to discos and parties?

a. Penny loafers
b. Cowboy boots
c. Platform shoes
d. Saddle shoes

6. Which of these movies came out in 1975?

a. The Poseidon Adventure
b. Jaws
c. The Towering Inferno
d. Rocky

7. Which 1976 song features the lyric "Is this the real life? Is this just fantasy?"

a. We Will Rock You
b. Another One Bites the Dust
c. Killer Queen
d. Bohemian Rhapsody

8. In 1971, which amendment to the U.S. Constitution officially lowered the voting age from 21 to 18?

a. 24th Amendment
b. 25th Amendment
c. 27th Amendment
d. 26th Amendment

9. In 1972, which U.S. swimmer won a record seven gold medals at the Munich Olympics?

a. Mark Spitz
b. Michael Phelps
c. Greg Louganis
d. Johnny Weissmuller

10. Which 1970s TV show featured the catchphrase "Dy-no-mite!"?

a. Sanford and Son
b. All in the Family
c. Happy Days
d. Good Times

11. In 1979, which British Prime Minister became the first woman to hold that office?

a. Theresa May
b. Angela Merkel
c. Margaret Thatcher
d. Indira Gandhi

12. Which 1970 song by Simon and Garfunkel became the title track of their final studio album together?

a. Mrs. Robinson
b. Scarborough Fair
c. The Boxer
d. Bridge Over Troubled Water

13. Which 1973 Supreme Court case legalized abortion nationwide in the United States?

a. Miranda v. Arizona
b. Tinker v. Des Moines
c. Brown v. Board of Education
d. Roe v. Wade

14. Which 1978 musical film starring John Travolta and Olivia Newton-John became a massive box office hit?

a. Saturday Night Fever
b. Fame
c. Grease
d. Cabaret

15. Which handheld electronic game, released in 1976, featured a simple LED football field and became one of the first portable sports games?

a. Atari Pong
b. Mattel Electronic Football
c. Game Boy
d. Coleco Head to Head

16. In 1974, which U.S. president became the only one to resign from office?

a. Lyndon B. Johnson
b. Gerald Ford
c. Jimmy Carter
d. Richard Nixon

17. Which 1971 album by Marvin Gaye is widely regarded as one of the greatest soul albums ever recorded?

a. Let's Get It On
b. Midnight Love
c. What's Going On
d. Talking Book

18. Which 1972 television series featured a Korean War medical unit and blended comedy with serious themes?

a. Hogan's Heroes
b. All in the Family
c. The Mary Tyler Moore Show
d. MASH

19. In 1973, which organization of oil producing nations announced an embargo that caused fuel shortages and long gas lines in the United States?

a. NATO
b. OPEC
c. The United Nations
d. The Federal Reserve

20. Which 1977 rock band formed in Dublin and later became one of the best selling bands of all time?

a. The Clash

b. AC/DC
c. U2
d. Fleetwood Mac

1. b) Star Wars - Released in 1977, it became the highest-grossing film of its time and launched a global franchise.

2. c) Bee Gees - Their disco era hits dominated the charts and dance floors throughout the late 1970s.

3. d) Watergate - The scandal led to congressional investigations and ultimately President Nixon's resignation.

4. d) Space Invaders - Released in 1978, it became one of the first worldwide arcade gaming sensations.

5. c) Platform shoes - Popular at discos and parties, they became one of the most recognizable fashion trends of the decade.

6. b) Jaws - The 1975 thriller became the first true summer blockbuster and changed Hollywood forever.

7. d) Bohemian Rhapsody - Queen's 1976 epic became one of the most iconic rock songs ever recorded.

8. d) 26th Amendment - Ratified in 1971, it officially lowered the voting age to 18 nationwide.

9. a) Mark Spitz - He won seven gold medals at the 1972 Munich Olympics, setting a record at the time.

10. d) Good Times - The catchphrase "Dy-no-mite!" became closely associated with the character J.J. Evans.

11. c) Margaret Thatcher - She became the first female Prime Minister of the United Kingdom in 1979.

12. d) Bridge Over Troubled Water - The 1970 title track became one of Simon and Garfunkel's biggest hits.

13. d) Roe v. Wade - The 1973 decision legalized abortion nationwide in the United States.

14. c) Grease - The 1978 musical became a major box office success and a lasting pop culture favorite.

15. b) Mattel Electronic Football - Released in 1976, it became one of the first popular handheld electronic games.

16. d) Richard Nixon - He resigned in 1974, becoming the only U.S. president to step down from office.

17. c) What's Going On - Released in 1971, it is widely regarded as one of the greatest soul albums ever made.

18. d) MASH - Premiering in 1972, it blended comedy and serious themes set during the Korean War.

19. b) OPEC - The 1973 oil embargo caused widespread fuel shortages and long lines at gas stations.

20. c) U2 - Formed in Dublin in 1977, the band went on to become one of the best-selling acts in music history.

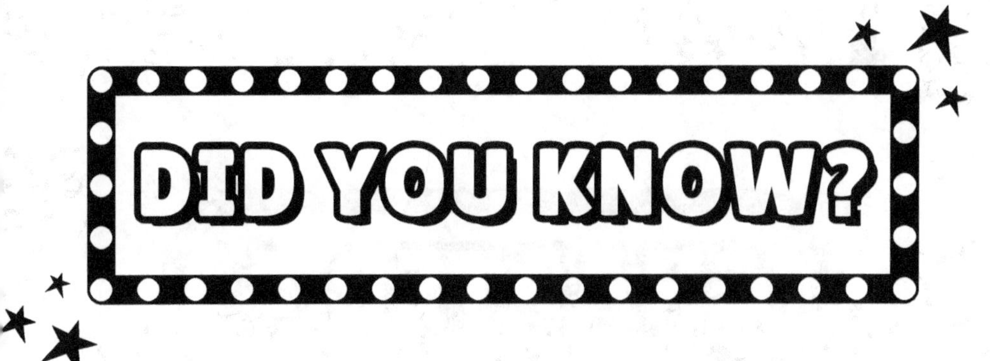

When Star Wars was being filmed in 1976, almost everyone involved, including the cast and crew, thought the movie would be a massive flop. The production went over budget by $3 million, and the studio had so little faith in it that they opened it in fewer than 40 theaters. Instead, it became a cultural phenomenon, grossing $410 million during its initial run.

The 1970s was a decade of incredible technological firsts that set the stage for the modern world. It saw the invention of the first digital camera, the first mobile phone, and the first microprocessor. Even everyday items we take for granted today, like the Post-it Note and the floppy disk, were born during this era of rapid innovation.

One of the most famous sports moments of the decade didn't happen on a field or court, but in a tennis stadium. The 1973 "Battle of the Sexes" tennis match between Billie Jean King and Bobby Riggs drew an estimated 90 million viewers worldwide. King's decisive victory became a landmark moment for women's sports.

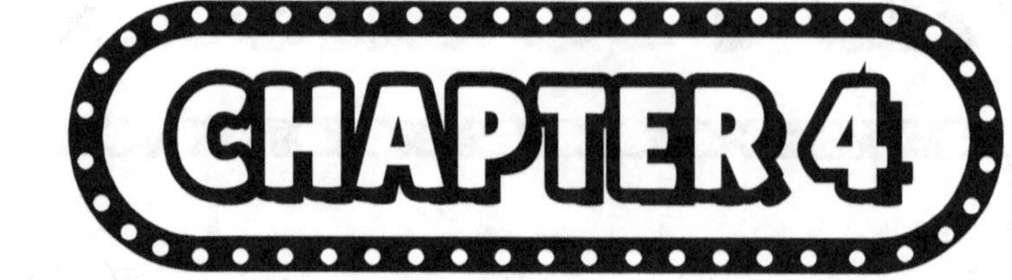

CHAPTER 4

Big Hair, Big Moments: The 80s

The 1980s were bright, bold, and turned up to full volume. It was a decade of big hair, big personalities, and technology that began transforming everyday life. Music videos played nonstop, blockbuster films filled theaters, and arcade games and home consoles brought competition into living rooms. Personal computers became more common, cable television expanded choices, and portable music players let people take their favorite songs anywhere. Fashion was loud, colorful, and unapologetic. From major political moments to unforgettable sports and pop culture icons, the 80s felt fast, energetic, and larger than life, leaving a lasting mark on music, entertainment, and global culture.

1. In 1981, which music television network launched and forever changed how people experienced popular music?

a. VH1
b. MTV
c. BET
d. CMT

2. In 1984, which film became the highest-grossing movie of the year and featured the character Axel Foley?

a. Beverly Hills Cop
b. Top Gun
c. Ghostbusters
d. Indiana Jones and the Temple of Doom

3. In 1983, which company manufactured the first commercially available handheld mobile phone, the DynaTAC 8000X?

a. Nokia
b. AT&T
c. Motorola
d. Ericsson

4. In 1987, which U.S. president delivered the speech at the Brandenburg Gate that included the line "Mr. Gorbachev, tear down this wall"?

a. Jimmy Carter

b. George H. W. Bush
c. Ronald Reagan
d. Gerald Ford

5. In 1980, Pac-Man was developed by which Japanese company before becoming a global arcade sensation?

a. Sega
b. Namco
c. Nintendo
d. Taito

6. In 1986, which space shuttle broke apart shortly after launch, leading to a nationwide period of mourning?

a. Columbia
b. Discovery
c. Challenger
d. Atlantis

7. Which 1982 Michael Jackson album became the best selling album of all time?

a. Off the Wall
b. Bad
c. Dangerous
d. Thriller

8. In 1984, which company introduced the first widely successful 3.5-inch floppy disk format?

a. IBM
b. Sony
c. Apple
d. Hewlett-Packard

9. Which 1983 video game crash severely impacted the North American home console market?

a. The Nintendo shortage
b. The Atari shortage
c. The Atari video game crash
d. The Sega recall

10. In 1988, which boxer defeated Michael Spinks in just 91 seconds to become the undisputed heavyweight champion?

a. Evander Holyfield
b. Larry Holmes
c. George Foreman
d. Mike Tyson

11. In 1982, which company released the first commercially successful home computer with a graphical user interface and mouse?

a. IBM
b. Commodore
c. Apple
d. Microsoft

12. In 1981, which professional sports league went on

strike, shortening its season and splitting it into two halves?
a. NBA
b. NFL
c. NHL
d. MLB

13. Which 1985 charity concert was held simultaneously in London and Philadelphia to raise funds for Ethiopian famine relief?

a. Farm Aid
b. We Are the World
c. Live Aid
d. Comic Relief

14. In 1987, which financial event became known as "Black Monday," causing one of the largest single-day percentage drops in stock market history?

a. The Savings and Loan Collapse
b. The Oil Shock
c. The Dot Com Bubble
d. The stock market crash

15. Which 1983 agreement between the United States and the Soviet Union aimed to reduce intermediate-range nuclear missiles in Europe?

a. SALT II
b. START I
c. The Helsinki Accords
d. INF Treaty

16. In 1985, which Japanese company released the Nintendo Entertainment System in the United States, revitalizing the home video game market after the 1983 crash?

a. Sega
b. Nintendo
c. Sony
d. Atari

17. In 1981, which British royal married Prince Charles in a globally televised ceremony watched by hundreds of millions?

a. Sarah Ferguson
b. Camilla Parker Bowles
c. Princess Anne
d. Lady Diana Spencer

18. In 1989, which environmental disaster occurred when an oil tanker ran aground in Alaska?

a. Three Mile Island
b. Love Canal
c. Exxon Valdez spill
d. Deepwater Horizon

19. Which novel by George Orwell regained massive popularity in the 1980s due to its themes of surveillance and totalitarianism?

a. Brave New World

b. Fahrenheit 451

c. Animal Farm

d. 1984

20. In 1986, which soccer legend led Argentina to victory in the World Cup and scored the controversial "Hand of God" goal?

a. Pele

b. Zico

c. Maradona

d. Platini

CHAPTER 4 ANSWERS

1. b) MTV - Launched in 1981, it revolutionized how audiences experienced music through nonstop music videos.

2. a) Beverly Hills Cop - It became the highest-grossing film of 1984 in the United States and made Eddie Murphy a major star.

3. c) Motorola - The DynaTAC 8000X, released in 1983, was the first commercially available handheld mobile phone.

4. c) Ronald Reagan - He delivered the famous "tear down this wall" speech in Berlin in 1987.

5. b) Namco - The Japanese company developed Pac-Man before it became a worldwide arcade sensation.

6. c) Challenger - The shuttle broke apart shortly after launch in 1986, shocking the nation.

7. d) Thriller - Released in 1982, it became the best-selling album of all time.

8. b) Sony - Sony introduced the widely successful 3.5-inch floppy disk format in the mid 1980s.

9. c) The Atari video game crash - The 1983 crash severely damaged the North American home console market.

10. d) Mike Tyson - In 1988, he defeated Michael Spinks in just 91 seconds.

11. c) Apple - The company released the Macintosh in 1984, the first commercially successful GUI home computer with a mouse.

12. d) MLB - The 1981 Major League Baseball strike split the season into two halves.

13. c) Live Aid - The 1985 concert was held simultaneously in London and Philadelphia to raise famine relief funds.

14. d) The stock market crash - Black Monday in 1987 caused one of the largest single-day percentage drops in market history.

15. d) INF Treaty - Signed in 1987, it reduced intermediate-range nuclear missiles in Europe.

16. b) Nintendo - The NES release in 1985 helped revive the home video game industry.

17. d) Lady Diana Spencer - She married Prince Charles in 1981 in a globally televised ceremony.

18. c) Exxon Valdez spill - The 1989 oil spill caused major environmental damage in Alaska.

19. d) 1984 - George Orwell's novel saw renewed popularity as the year 1984 approached.

20. c) Maradona - He led Argentina to victory in the 1986 World Cup and scored the infamous "Hand of God" goal.

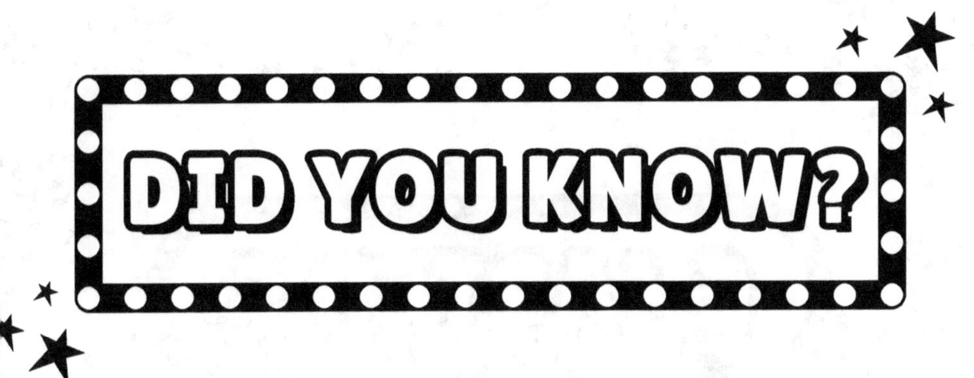

MTV launched on August 1, 1981, with a simple mission: to play music videos 24 hours a day. The network's first video ever broadcast was "Video Killed the Radio Star" by The Buggles, setting the tone for a decade where visual presentation became just as important as the music itself.

The 1980s witnessed a personal computer revolution that fundamentally changed how people worked and communicated. The IBM PC arrived in 1981, followed by the Apple II and Commodore 64, bringing computing power into homes and small businesses for the first time.

The decade also saw the rise of blockbuster action movies and the birth of the modern superhero film era. Directors like Steven Spielberg and George Lucas continued to dominate the box office, while new franchises like "The Terminator" and "Back to the Future" became instant classics. The 1980s proved that audiences had an insatiable appetite for spectacular special effects and larger-than-life entertainment.

CHAPTER 5

The Fast-Changing 90s

The 1990s felt like a bridge between two worlds. The decade began with cassette tapes, video rental stores, and landline phones, and ended with email and search engines. The internet shifted from a curiosity to a daily tool, changing how people worked, shopped, and stayed connected. Music moved from grunge to pop superstars, blockbuster films filled theaters, and video game consoles became staples in living rooms. Cable news ran nonstop as global shifts reshaped politics and alliances. Yet everyday life still had a slower rhythm, with plans made without text messages, photos developed instead of uploaded, and evenings spent around a favorite show or on a trip to the mall. The 1990s blended simplicity with rapid change, setting the stage for the digital world that followed.

1. In 1991, which music video by Nirvana helped push grunge into the mainstream?

a. Come As You Are
b. Heart-Shaped Box
c. Smells Like Teen Spirit
d. Lithium

2. Which 1997 film became the highest-grossing movie of the decade?

a. Jurassic Park
b. Forrest Gump
c. Independence Day
d. Titanic

3. In 1995, which company launched a massive marketing campaign featuring the Rolling Stones song "Start Me Up"?

a. Apple
b. IBM
c. Microsoft
d. Intel

4. Which 1992 sporting event featured the legendary U.S. "Dream Team" basketball roster?

a. Atlanta Olympics
b. Barcelona Olympics
c. Sydney Olympics
d. Seoul Olympics

5. Which handheld gaming device, released in the early 1990s, popularized games like Tetris and Pokemon?

a. Sega Game Gear
b. Atari Lynx
c. PlayStation Portable
d. Game Boy

6. In 1994, which former football star was involved in a highly publicized police chase in a white Ford Bronco?

a. Dan Marino
b. John Elway
c. O.J. Simpson
d. Troy Aikman

7. Which 1999 science fiction film featured the line "There is no spoon"?

a. The Fifth Element
b. Blade Runner
c. The Matrix
d. Minority Report

8. In 1990, which German tennis star won Wimbledon and became one of the biggest sports icons of the decade?

a. Stefan Edberg
b. Boris Becker
c. Andre Agassi
d. Pete Sampras

9. Which search engine company was founded in 1998?

a. Yahoo
b. Ask Jeeves
c. Netscape
d. Google

10. In 1991, which country officially dissolved, marking the end of the Cold War era?

a. Yugoslavia
b. Czechoslovakia
c. East Germany
d. The Soviet Union

11. In 1994, which country held its first fully democratic elections, leading to Nelson Mandela becoming president?

a. Zimbabwe
b. Kenya
c. South Africa
d. Ghana

12. Which 1991 album by Metallica is often referred to simply as "The Black Album"?

a. Master of Puppets
b. Ride the Lightning
c. Kill 'Em All
d. Metallica

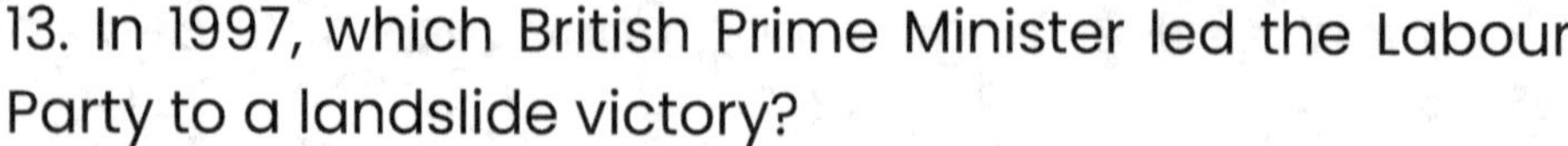

13. In 1997, which British Prime Minister led the Labour Party to a landslide victory?

a. John Major
b. Tony Blair
c. Gordon Brown
d. David Cameron

14. Which 1993 peace agreement was signed on the White House lawn between Israel and the PLO?

a. Camp David Accords
b. Dayton Agreement
c. Oslo Accords
d. Good Friday Agreement

15. In 1998, which Major League Baseball player broke Roger Maris's single-season home run record?

a. Sammy Sosa
b. Barry Bonds
c. Ken Griffey Jr.
d. Mark McGwire

16. Which 1995 crime film directed by David Fincher ends with the line "What's in the box?"

a. Pulp Fiction
b. The Usual Suspects
c. Heat
d. Se7en

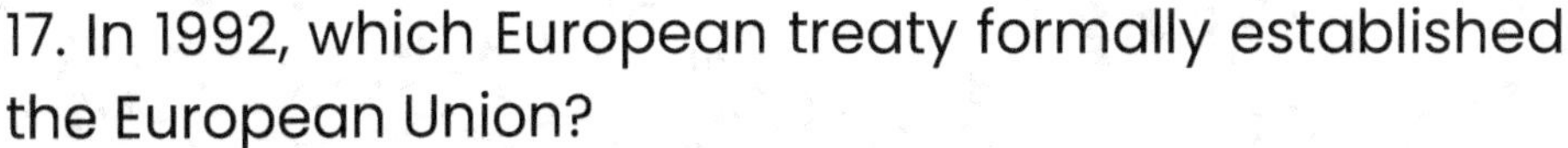

17. In 1992, which European treaty formally established the European Union?

a. Treaty of Rome
b. Schengen Agreement
c. Maastricht Treaty
d. Lisbon Treaty

18. Which 1996 video game introduced players to the character Lara Croft?

a. Resident Evil
b. Tomb Raider
c. Silent Hill
d. Final Fantasy VII

19. In 1996, which telecommunications company popularized the slogan "Can you hear me now?"

a. AT&T
b. Sprint
c. T-Mobile
d. Verizon

20. Which 1999 conflict involved NATO airstrikes in the Balkans?

a. Gulf War
b. Bosnian War
c. Kosovo War
d. Chechen War

CHAPTER 5 ANSWERS

1. c) Smells Like Teen Spirit - The 1991 video helped bring grunge into the mainstream and defined early 90s alternative rock.

2. d) Titanic - Released in 1997, it became the highest-grossing film of the decade and won 11 Academy Awards.

3. c) Microsoft - The company used the Rolling Stones song "Start Me Up" to launch Windows 95.

4. b) Barcelona Olympics - The 1992 games featured the legendary U.S. "Dream Team" basketball roster.

5. d) Game Boy - Nintendo's handheld device made portable gaming hugely popular in the early 1990s.

6. c) O.J. Simpson - The 1994 police chase in a white Ford Bronco became one of the most watched live television events of the decade.

7. c) The Matrix - The 1999 film became iconic for its groundbreaking effects and memorable quotes.

8. b) Boris Becker - The German tennis star was one of the most recognizable sports figures of the early 1990s.

9. d) Google - Founded in 1998, it quickly became the dominant search engine on the internet.

10. d) The Soviet Union - Its dissolution in 1991 marked the official end of the Cold War.

11. c) South Africa - The 1994 election led to Nelson Mandela becoming the country's first Black president.

12. d) Metallica - The 1991 self-titled album became known as "The Black Album" and was a massive commercial success.

13. b) Tony Blair - He led the Labour Party to a landslide victory in the 1997 UK general election.

14. c) Oslo Accords - The 1993 agreement was signed at the White House between Israel and the PLO.

15. d) Mark McGwire - He broke Roger Maris's single-season home run record in 1998.

16. d) Se7en - The 1995 thriller is remembered for its shocking ending and that famous line.

17. c) Maastricht Treaty - Signed in 1992, it formally established the European Union.

18. b) Tomb Raider - Released in 1996, it introduced the world to Lara Croft, who quickly became one of the most recognizable video game characters of the 1990s.

19. d) Verizon - The slogan "Can you hear me now?" became widely recognized in the late 1990s and early 2000s.

20. c) Kosovo War - The 1999 conflict involved NATO airstrikes in the Balkans.

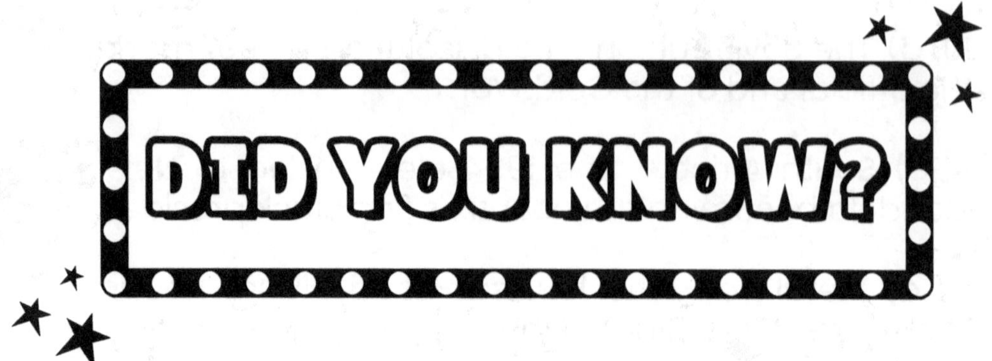

The World Wide Web, invented by British scientist Tim Berners-Lee in 1989, became publicly available in the early 1990s and forever changed human communication and information sharing. The first web browser, called WorldWideWeb, was released on Christmas Day 1990, but it wasn't until the mid-1990s that the internet truly exploded into mainstream consciousness.

Grunge music emerged from Seattle in the early 1990s and became a cultural phenomenon that defined the decade. Nirvana's 1991 album "Nevermind" and its hit single "Smells Like Teen Spirit" catapulted the genre into the mainstream, making flannel shirts and angst-ridden lyrics the uniform of youth culture. The movement represented a rejection of the excess and materialism of the 1980s.

The 1990s also marked the birth of reality television as we know it. "The Real World" premiered on MTV in 1992, becoming the first true reality television series and launching a completely new genre. The show followed seven strangers living together in a New York loft, and its success proved that audiences were fascinated by watching ordinary people navigate real-life drama.

CHAPTER 6

A New Millennium: The 2000s

The 2000s began with uncertainty and ended in transformation. It was a decade of rapid technological change and a world that felt more connected than ever. News traveled instantly, phones became smarter, and the internet became part of daily life. Social media emerged, reality television grew, and blockbuster films filled theaters. Music shifted from CDs to digital downloads, and shopping moved online. The 2000s reshaped communication and entertainment, setting the stage for the connected world that followed.

1. In 2002, which singing competition show crowned Kelly Clarkson as its first winner?

a. The Voice
b. American Idol
c. The X Factor
d. Popstars

2. In 2007, which U.S. telecom carrier was the exclusive launch partner for the first iPhone?

a. Verizon
b. Sprint
c. AT&T
d. T-Mobile

3. At the 2007 iPhone keynote, Steve Jobs famously described the device as combining three products. Which of the following was NOT one of them?

a. A widescreen iPod
b. A revolutionary mobile phone
c. An internet communicator
d. A digital camera

4. In 2003, which film became the first fantasy movie to win the Academy Award for Best Picture?

a. Harry Potter and the Chamber of Secrets
b. The Chronicles of Narnia: The Lion, the Witch and the Wardrobe

c. The Lord of the Rings: The Return of the King
d. Pirates of the Caribbean: The Curse of the Black Pearl

5. Which social media platform, founded in 2004, was originally limited to college students?

a. MySpace
b. Twitter
c. LinkedIn
d. Facebook

6. In 2000, which dot com crash led to massive losses in technology stocks?

a. Housing bubble
b. Dot com bubble burst
c. Savings and Loan crisis
d. Subprime mortgage collapse

7. Which 2009 pop singer released the album "The Fame Monster" featuring hits like "Bad Romance"?

a. Britney Spears
b. Rihanna
c. Beyonce
d. Lady Gaga

8. In 2003, which country did the United States invade in a war that led to the overthrow of Saddam Hussein?

a. Afghanistan

b. Iran
c. Iraq
d. Syria

9. Which video game console, released in 2006, introduced motion controls with a handheld remote?

a. PlayStation 3
b. Xbox 360
c. Nintendo Wii
d. Sega Dreamcast

10. In 2005, which hurricane caused catastrophic damage to New Orleans?

a. Sandy
b. Andrew
c. Harvey
d. Katrina

11. In 2005, which religious leader passed away after serving as head of the Catholic Church for more than 25 years?

a. Pope Benedict XVI
b. Pope John Paul II
c. Pope Francis
d. Archbishop Desmond Tutu

12. In 2008, which major U.S. investment bank collapsed, becoming the largest bankruptcy filing in American history at the time?

a. Goldman Sachs
b. Morgan Stanley
c. Lehman Brothers
d. Bear Stearns

13. In the 2008 Beijing Olympics, which swimmer won a record eight gold medals in a single Games?

a. Ian Thorpe
b. Mark Spitz
c. Ryan Lochte
d. Michael Phelps

14. Which 2007 book became the final installment in the original Harry Potter series?

a. Harry Potter and the Half-Blood Prince
b. Harry Potter and the Goblet of Fire
c. Harry Potter and the Order of the Phoenix
d. Harry Potter and the Deathly Hallows

15. In 2000, which Russian leader first became president?

a. Dmitry Medvedev
b. Vladimir Putin
c. Boris Yeltsin
d. Mikhail Gorbachev

16. Which online video platform, founded in 2005, allowed users to upload and share videos easily?

a. Vimeo
b. MySpace
c. Dailymotion
d. YouTube

17. In 2006, which company purchased Pixar Animation Studios?

a. DreamWorks
b. Warner Bros.
c. Sony
d. Disney

18. Which 2009 film became the highest grossing movie of all time at that point?

a. The Dark Knight
b. Titanic
c. Transformers
d. Avatar

19. In 2004, which Asian nation was devastated by a massive Indian Ocean tsunami?

a. Japan
b. China
c. Indonesia
d. Thailand

20. In 2008, which company's CEO famously introduced the first Android powered smartphone, the T-Mobile G1?

a. Steve Jobs
b. Bill Gates
c. Andy Rubin
d. Jeff Bezos

1. b) American Idol – Kelly Clarkson became the first winner in 2002, launching one of the biggest TV talent franchises of the decade.

2. c) AT&T – The first iPhone in 2007 was exclusively sold through AT&T in the United States at launch.

3. d) A digital camera – At the 2007 iPhone keynote, Steve Jobs described the device as combining a widescreen iPod, a revolutionary mobile phone, and an internet communicator, but not a digital camera.

4. c) The Lord of the Rings: The Return of the King – The 2003 film swept the Academy Awards and was the first fantasy movie to win Best Picture.

5. d) Facebook – Founded in 2004 and initially limited to college students before expanding globally.

6. b) Dot com bubble burst – The early 2000s saw the collapse of many technology stocks following the dot com crash.

7. d) Lady Gaga – Her 2009 album The Fame Monster included hits like "Bad Romance."

8. c) Iraq – In 2003, the U.S. led an invasion of Iraq that resulted in the overthrow of Saddam Hussein's regime.

9. c) Nintendo Wii – Released in 2006 with its innovative handheld motion-sensing controller.

10. d) Katrina – Hurricane Katrina caused devastating damage in New Orleans and the Gulf Coast in 2005.

11. b) Pope John Paul II – He passed away in 2005 after more than 25 years as head of the Catholic Church.

12. c) Lehman Brothers – Its 2008 collapse was the largest bankruptcy in U.S. history at the time and a key moment in the financial crisis.

13. d) Michael Phelps – He won eight gold medals at the 2008 Beijing Olympics, setting a record.

14. d) Harry Potter and the Deathly Hallows – The 2007 book was the final installment in the original Harry Potter series.

15. b) Vladimir Putin – He first became president of Russia in 2000.

16. d) YouTube – Founded in 2005, it became a dominant platform for sharing online video.

17. d) Disney – The company purchased Pixar Animation Studios in 2006.

18. d) Avatar – The 2009 film became the highest grossing movie of all time at that point.

19. c) Indonesia – It was one of the countries devastated by the 2004 Indian Ocean tsunami.

20. c) Andy Rubin – He was the creator of the Android operating system that powered the first Android smartphone, the T-Mobile G1, in 2008.

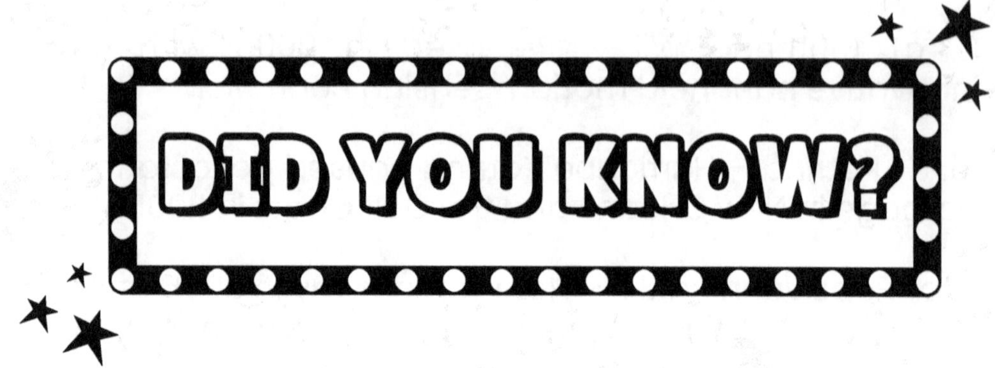

The early 2000s saw the rise of social media platforms that would reshape how people connect and communicate. MySpace dominated the mid-2000s as the world's most visited social networking site, allowing users to customize their profiles with music and graphics. However, Facebook's expansion beyond college campuses in 2006 eventually overtook MySpace, introducing a cleaner interface and real-name culture that would become the standard for social networks worldwide.

YouTube was initially envisioned in part as a video dating site when it launched in 2005, but it quickly evolved into the world's largest video-sharing platform. Within just a few years, YouTube became so influential that it fundamentally changed how people consume entertainment, allowing anyone with a camera to become a content creator. The platform's impact on culture, music, and politics cannot be overstated, as it democratized media production in ways that were previously unimaginable.

The 2000s also witnessed the explosion of the iPod and digital music. At its peak in 2008, Apple sold over 54 million iPods in a single year, accounting for around 40 percent of the company's total revenue. This shift from physical media to digital downloads represented a seismic change in how people consumed music, ultimately leading to the streaming services that dominate today's music industry.

CHAPTER 7

A Connected World: The 2010s

The 2010s were defined by constant connection and rapid change. Smartphones became part of everyday life, social media shaped conversations in real time, and streaming transformed how people watched TV and movies. Viral moments spread instantly, music moved to digital platforms, and blockbuster franchises dominated theaters. Technology blurred the line between public and private life, while cultural movements sparked global conversation. The 2010s felt fast, interactive, and more connected than ever before.

1. In 2013, which social media platform introduced the "Stories" feature that would later be widely copied by other apps?

a. Facebook
b. Snapchat
c. Twitter
d. LinkedIn

2. In 2016, which country voted in a referendum to leave the European Union?

a. France
b. Greece
c. United Kingdom
d. Italy

3. Which 2013 film won the Academy Award for Best Picture and was based on the true story of Solomon Northup?

a. The King's Speech
b. Lincoln
c. Argo
d. 12 Years a Slave

4. In 2012, which spacecraft successfully landed the Curiosity rover on Mars using a "sky crane" maneuver?

a. Apollo
b. Voyager
c. NASA
d. SpaceX

5. Which 2018 sporting event saw France defeat Croatia in the final?

a. UEFA Euro
b. Champions League
c. Copa America
d. FIFA World Cup

6. In 2011, which Middle Eastern uprisings became known collectively as a major wave of protests across the region?

a. The Green Movement
b. The Arab Spring
c. The Cedar Revolution
d. The Intifada

7. Which 2019 film became the highest grossing movie of all time, surpassing Avatar?

a. Avengers: Infinity War
b. Star Wars: The Rise of Skywalker
c. Avengers: Endgame
d. Jurassic World

8. In 2014, which global health crisis centered around an outbreak in West Africa?

a. SARS
b. Swine flu
c. Zika virus
d. Ebola

9. Which streaming platform, originally known for mailing DVDs, became a dominant force in original television content during the 2010s?

a. Hulu
b. Amazon Prime Video
c. Disney+
d. Netflix

10. In 2013, which former NSA contractor revealed classified surveillance programs, sparking worldwide debate over privacy?

a. Julian Assange
b. Chelsea Manning
c. Edward Snowden
d. Mark Felt

11. In 2015, which international agreement aimed to limit global temperature rise and address climate change?

a. Kyoto Protocol
b. Copenhagen Accord
c. Paris Agreement
d. Geneva Climate Pact

12. In 2012, which social media platform was acquired by Facebook for approximately $1 billion?

a. Snapchat
b. Instagram
c. Tumblr

c. Pinterest

13. In 2018, which company became the first to reach a $1 trillion market valuation?

a. Microsoft
b. Amazon
c. Google
d. Apple

14. In 2014, which country annexed Crimea, leading to widespread international sanctions?

a. Turkey
b. China
c. Russia
d. Iran

15. Which 2016 music artist released the album "Lemonade," which was accompanied by a full visual film?

a. Rihanna
b. Adele
c. Taylor Swift
d. Beyonce

16. In 2008 which company launched a streaming music service that helped accelerate the decline of digital music downloads?
a. Pandora
b. Apple
c. Spotify

d. SoundCloud

17. In 2017, which cryptocurrency surged dramatically in value, bringing blockchain technology into mainstream conversation?

a. Ethereum
b. Litecoin
c. Ripple
d. Bitcoin

18. In 2013, which British Prime Minister announced a referendum on European Union membership that would later lead to Brexit?

a. Gordon Brown
b. Tony Blair
c. David Cameron
d. Theresa May

19. In 2013, which future king of the United Kingdom was born, becoming third in line to the throne at the time?

a. Prince Harry
b. Prince Andrew
c. Prince George
d. Prince Edward

20. In 2014, which extremist group declared a "caliphate" across parts of Iraq and Syria?

a. Al-Qaeda
b. Taliban
c. Boko Haram
d. ISIS

1. b) Snapchat – It introduced the "Stories" feature in 2013, which was later copied by multiple platforms.

2. c) United Kingdom – The 2016 Brexit referendum resulted in a vote to leave the European Union.

3. d) 12 Years a Slave – The 2013 film won Best Picture and was based on Solomon Northup's memoir.

4. c) NASA – NASA's Curiosity rover landed on Mars in 2012 using the innovative "sky crane" maneuver.

5. d) FIFA World Cup – France defeated Croatia in the 2018 World Cup final.

6. b) The Arab Spring – A wave of protests and uprisings spread across the Middle East beginning in 2011.

7. c) Avengers: Endgame – The 2019 film surpassed Avatar to become the highest grossing movie at that time.

8. d) Ebola – The 2014 outbreak in West Africa became a major global health crisis.

9. d) Netflix – Originally a DVD by mail service, it became a dominant streaming platform in the 2010s.

10. c) Edward Snowden – He revealed classified NSA surveillance programs in 2013.

11. c) Paris Agreement – The 2015 international accord aimed to limit global temperature rise.

12. b) Instagram – Facebook acquired Instagram in 2012 for approximately $1 billion.

13. d) Apple – In 2018, Apple became the first publicly traded company to reach a $1 trillion valuation.

14. c) Russia – Russia annexed Crimea in 2014, prompting international sanctions.

15. d) Beyonce – Her 2016 album "Lemonade" was released alongside a full visual film.

16. c) Spotify – Launched in the 2008, it accelerated the shift from downloads to streaming.

17. d) Bitcoin – Its dramatic price surge in 2017 brought cryptocurrency into mainstream conversation.

18. c) David Cameron – He announced the EU referendum that ultimately led to Brexit.

19. c) Prince George – Born in 2013, he became third in line to the British throne at the time.

20. d) ISIS – The group declared a caliphate across parts of Iraq and Syria in 2014.

The 2010s saw the rise of Instagram and Snapchat as the dominant social media platforms for younger generations. Instagram, which launched in 2010, became synonymous with the decade's image-driven culture and the rise of influencers as a new form of celebrity. Snapchat's ephemeral messaging and innovative filters created a new way for people to share moments, and by the mid-2010s, especially from 2014 to 2017, Snapchat dominated youth culture in ways that defined the era.

Netflix's transformation from a DVD rental service to a streaming giant fundamentally changed how people watched television and movies. The concept of "binge-watching" entire seasons of shows became the norm, with Netflix originals like "House of Cards," "Orange is the New Black," and "Stranger Things" becoming cultural phenomena. This shift disrupted the entire entertainment industry, forcing traditional networks and studios to rethink their business models.

The 2010s also saw the continued evolution of technology and social consciousness. Lady Gaga's infamous meat dress at the 2010 MTV Video Music Awards became one of the decade's most iconic pop culture moments. The decade proved that technology and culture were increasingly intertwined.

CHAPTER 8

Lights, Camera, Action: TV & Movie Memories

Before streaming and on-demand options, television and movies were shared events. Families gathered at set times to watch their favorite shows, and movie premieres filled theaters with excitement. Theme songs were instantly recognizable, catchphrases were repeated everywhere, and characters felt like part of the family. From classic sitcoms to blockbuster films, these stories shaped culture and conversation. Think you remember the golden age of TV and film? Let's find out.

1. Which actor played Archie Bunker on the television series "All in the Family"?

a. Carroll O'Connor
b. Alan Alda
c. Redd Foxx
d. Jackie Gleason

2. In the television series "MASH," which actor portrayed Hawkeye Pierce?

a. Mike Farrell
b. Alan Alda
c. Donald Sutherland
d. Gary Burghoff

3. Which 1972 film featured the famous line, "I'm gonna make him an offer he can't refuse"?

a. Goodfellas
b. The French Connection
c. The Godfather
d. Scarface

4. Which actress starred as Mary Richards in "The Mary Tyler Moore Show"?

a. Cloris Leachman
b. Valerie Harper
c. Mary Tyler Moore
d. Carol Burnett

5. In "Happy Days," which actor played Arthur "The Fonz" Fonzarelli?

a. Ron Howard
b. Henry Winkler
c. Scott Baio
d. Anson Williams

6. Which 1965 film starred Julie Andrews as Maria, a governess to the Von Trapp children?

a. My Fair Lady
b. Camelot
c. The Sound of Music
d. West Side Story

7. Which actor portrayed Detective Columbo in the long-running television series?

a. Telly Savalas
b. Peter Falk
c. Jack Klugman
d. Robert Stack

8. In the original "Star Trek" series, which actor played Captain James T. Kirk?

a. Leonard Nimoy
b. Patrick Stewart
c. William Shatner
d. George Takei

9. Which 1984 film featured Eddie Murphy as a fast talking Detroit police officer in Los Angeles?

a. Trading Places
b. 48 Hrs.
c. Beverly Hills Cop
d. Coming to America

10. Which actress played Scarlett O'Hara in the 1939 film "Gone with the Wind"?

a. Bette Davis
b. Vivien Leigh
c. Olivia de Havilland
d. Ingrid Bergman

11. Which actor played Tony Soprano in the television series "The Sopranos"?

a. Al Pacino
b. James Gandolfini
c. Robert De Niro
d. Ray Liotta

12. In the film "Jaws," which actor portrayed Police Chief Martin Brody?

a. Roy Scheider
b. Robert Shaw
c. Richard Dreyfuss
d. Richard Harris

13. Which actress starred opposite Humphrey Bogart in the 1942 film "Casablanca"?

a. Katharine Hepburn
b. Ava Gardner
c. Ingrid Bergman
d. Lauren Bacall

14. On "The Andy Griffith Show," who played Sheriff Andy Taylor?

a. Don Knotts
b. Jim Nabors
c. Andy Griffith
d. Ron Howard

15. Which 1977 film earned eleven Academy Award nominations and won seven, including Best Original Score for John Williams?

a. Saturday Night Fever
b. Star Wars
c. Close Encounters of the Third Kind
d. Annie Hall

16. Which actor played Indiana Jones in the original film trilogy?

a. Tom Selleck
b. Mel Gibson
c. Harrison Ford
d. Kurt Russell

17. In the sitcom "I Love Lucy," who played Lucy Ricardo?

a. Carol Burnett
b. Lucille Ball
c. Mary Tyler Moore
d. Elizabeth Montgomery

18. Which actor portrayed Rocky Balboa in the original 1976 film?

a. Robert De Niro
b. Al Pacino
c. Sylvester Stallone
d. Burt Reynolds

19. Which 1968 film featured Charlton Heston discovering the Statue of Liberty in its final scene?

a. 2001: A Space Odyssey
b. Soylent Green
c. Planet of the Apes
d. The Omega Man

20. Which actress played Princess Leia in the original "Star Wars" trilogy?

a. Sigourney Weaver
b. Carrie Fisher
c. Linda Hamilton
d. Glenn Close

CHAPTER 8
ANSWERS

1. a) Carroll O'Connor – He brought Archie Bunker to life in "All in the Family," one of the most iconic sitcom characters in television history.

2. b) Alan Alda – Alda portrayed Hawkeye Pierce throughout the long-running series "MASH."

3. c) The Godfather – The famous line is spoken by Marlon Brando's character, Don Vito Corleone.

4. c) Mary Tyler Moore – She starred as Mary Richards in the groundbreaking sitcom.

5. b) Henry Winkler – Winkler played the cool and unforgettable "Fonz" on "Happy Days."

6. c) The Sound of Music – Julie Andrews starred as Maria in the beloved 1965 musical film.

7. b) Peter Falk – He portrayed the rumpled but brilliant Detective Columbo.

8. c) William Shatner – He played Captain James T. Kirk in the original "Star Trek" series.

9. c) Beverly Hills Cop – Eddie Murphy starred as Axel Foley in the 1984 hit film.

10. b) Vivien Leigh – She played Scarlett O'Hara in the 1939 classic "Gone with the Wind."

11. b) James Gandolfini – He portrayed Tony Soprano in the acclaimed HBO series.

12. a) Roy Scheider – He played Police Chief Martin Brody in "Jaws."

13. c) Ingrid Bergman – She starred opposite Humphrey Bogart in "Casablanca."

14. c) Andy Griffith – He played Sheriff Andy Taylor on "The Andy Griffith Show."

15. b) Star Wars – The 1977 film earned eleven Oscar nominations and won seven.

16. c) Harrison Ford – He starred as Indiana Jones in the original trilogy.

17. b) Lucille Ball – She played Lucy Ricardo in the classic sitcom "I Love Lucy."

18. c) Sylvester Stallone – He created and portrayed Rocky Balboa in the 1976 film.

19. c) Planet of the Apes – The film ends with Charlton Heston discovering the Statue of Liberty.

20. b) Carrie Fisher – She portrayed Princess Leia in the original "Star Wars" trilogy.

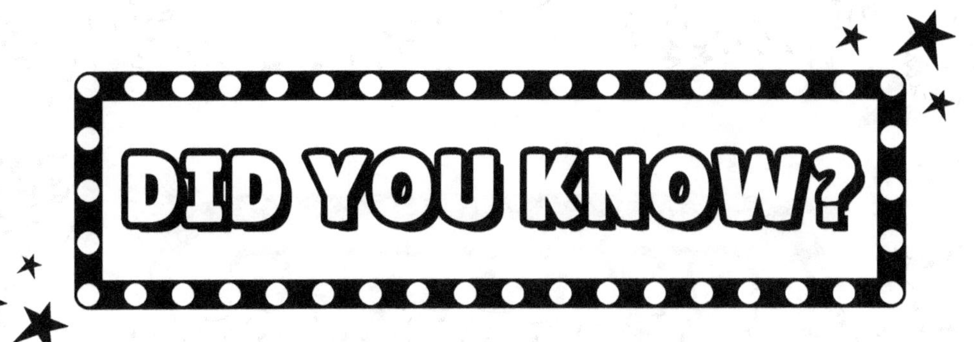

"I Love Lucy," which premiered on October 15, 1951, is widely considered one of the greatest television shows of all time and was voted the best TV show ever in a 2012 survey (conducted by ABC News and People magazine). The show, starring Lucille Ball and Desi Arnaz, revolutionized television by being one of the first sitcoms to be filmed in front of a live audience. The show's influence on comedy and television production techniques cannot be overstated, as it established many of the conventions that sitcoms still follow today.

The Golden Age of Hollywood, spanning from the 1930s through the 1960s, produced some of cinema's most enduring classics. During this era, the five major studios (MGM, Paramount, Fox, Warner Bros., and RKO) controlled nearly every aspect of filmmaking, from production to distribution. This system produced legendary films and stars, though it also enforced strict control over actors' public images and personal lives in ways that would be unthinkable today.

Films are almost universally projected at 24 frames per second, a standard that has remained virtually unchanged since the early days of cinema. This frame rate is just above the threshold of what the human eye can perceive as individual frames (around 13 fps), creating the illusion of smooth motion. This technical standard, established over a century ago, continues to define how movies look and feel, demonstrating how early technological decisions can have lasting impacts on an entire medium.

CHAPTER 9

Champions & Headlines: Sports & World Moments

Some moments go far beyond the scoreboard. They stop conversations, fill living rooms, and bring entire countries to their feet. Whether it was an underdog victory, a record-breaking performance, or a dramatic finish, these were the moments people remember exactly where they were. For decades, major sporting triumphs and historic events have united millions in front of screens and radios. From Olympic glory and long-awaited championships to shocking upsets and unforgettable celebrations, these were shared experiences that became part of cultural memory. This chapter revisits the moments that defined an era.

1. In 1980, which U.S. Olympic hockey victory became known as the "Miracle on Ice"?

a. USA defeating Canada
b. USA defeating Sweden
c. USA defeating the Soviet Union
d. USA defeating Finland

2. In 1994, which country hosted the FIFA World Cup for the first time?

a. Germany
b. Mexico
c. United States
d. Brazil

3. Which boxer defeated George Foreman in 1974 in the famous "Rumble in the Jungle"?

a. Joe Frazier
b. Larry Holmes
c. Muhammad Ali
d. Mike Tyson

4. In 1997, which NBA team won its fifth championship of the decade?

a. Los Angeles Lakers
b. Boston Celtics
c. Detroit Pistons
d. Chicago Bulls

5. Which tennis legend won 20 Grand Slam singles titles before retiring in 2022?

a. Novak Djokovic
b. Pete Sampras
c. Roger Federer
d. Andre Agassi

6. In 1998, which country won the FIFA World Cup on home soil?

a. Germany
b. Brazil
c. France
d. Italy

7. Which NFL quarterback led the New England Patriots to six Super Bowl victories?

a. Joe Montana
b. Peyton Manning
c. Terry Bradshaw
d. Tom Brady

8. In 2000, which major championship did Tiger Woods win by a record 15 strokes?

a. The Masters
b. The U.S. Open
c. The Open Championship
d. The PGA Championship

9. In 1999, which U.S. women's soccer player famously removed her jersey in celebration after scoring the winning penalty in the World Cup final?

a. Mia Hamm
b. Abby Wambach
c. Brandi Chastain
d. Julie Foudy

10. In 1988, which sprinter was stripped of his Olympic gold medal after testing positive for performance enhancing drugs?

a. Carl Lewis
b. Linford Christie
c. Maurice Greene
d. Ben Johnson

11. In 1985, which NBA team selected Michael Jordan with the third overall pick in the draft?

a. Los Angeles Lakers
b. Boston Celtics
c. Detroit Pistons
d. Chicago Bulls

12. In 2004, which baseball team ended an 86-year championship drought known as the "Curse of the Bambino"?

a. Chicago Cubs
b. New York Yankees
c. Boston Red Sox

d. Los Angeles Dodgers

13. Which female tennis player was the first African American player to win a Grand Slam title, winning the U.S. National Championships in 1957?

a. Venus Williams
b. Serena Williams
c. Billie Jean King
d. Althea Gibson

14. In 1972, which chess player defeated Boris Spassky in a Cold War era match known as the "Match of the Century"?

a. Garry Kasparov
b. Anatoly Karpov
c. Bobby Fischer
d. Magnus Carlsen

15. In 2016, which baseball team ended a 108 year championship drought, winning its first World Series since 1908?

a. Cleveland Indians
b. Boston Red Sox
c. Chicago Cubs
d. Los Angeles Dodgers

16. In 1998, which home run race between two players captivated the United States during the baseball season?

a. Ken Griffey Jr. and Barry Bonds
b. Mark McGwire and Sammy Sosa
c. Derek Jeter and Alex Rodriguez
d. Cal Ripken Jr. and Roger Clemens

17. In 1973, which horse won the Triple Crown, becoming one of the most celebrated racehorses in history?

a. Secretariat
b. Seattle Slew
c. Affirmed
d. Kelso

18. In 1996, which gymnast scored a dramatic vault despite an injured ankle to help secure Olympic gold for the United States?

a. Shannon Miller
b. Dominique Dawes
c. Mary Lou Retton
d. Kerri Strug

19. In 1984, which athlete set a record by winning four gold medals in track and field at a single Olympic Games?

a. Carl Lewis
b. Edwin Moses
c. Michael Johnson
d. Jesse Owens

20. In 2008, which U.S. gymnast returned to competition to win a team silver medal after being initially left off the Olympic roster?

a. Shawn Johnson
b. Dominique Dawes
c. Chelsie Memmel
d. Nastia Liukin

CHAPTER 9 ANSWERS

1. c) USA defeating the Soviet Union – The 1980 Olympic hockey victory became known as the "Miracle on Ice."

2. c) United States – The U.S. hosted the FIFA World Cup for the first time in 1994.

3. c) Muhammad Ali – He defeated George Foreman in the 1974 "Rumble in the Jungle."

4. d) Chicago Bulls – They won their fifth championship of the 1990s in 1997.

5. c) Roger Federer – He retired in 2022 with 20 Grand Slam singles titles.

6. c) France – France won the 1998 World Cup on home soil.

7. d) Tom Brady – He led the New England Patriots to six Super Bowl victories.

8. b) The U.S. Open – Tiger Woods won it by a record 15 strokes in 2000.

9. c) Brandi Chastain – She famously removed her jersey after scoring the winning penalty in 1999.

10. d) Ben Johnson – He was stripped of his Olympic gold medal in 1988 after testing positive.

11. d) Chicago Bulls – They selected Michael Jordan third overall in 1985.

12. c) Boston Red Sox – They ended their 86 year championship drought in 2004.

13. d) Althea Gibson – She became the first African American woman to win a Grand Slam title in the Open Era.

14. c) Bobby Fischer – He defeated Boris Spassky in the 1972 "Match of the Century."

15. c) Chicago Cubs – They ended their 108 year drought by winning the 2016 World Series.

16. b) Mark McGwire and Sammy Sosa – Their 1998 home run race captivated the nation.

17. a) Secretariat – He won the Triple Crown in 1973.

18. d) Kerri Strug – She landed her vault on an injured ankle in the 1996 Olympics.

19. a) Carl Lewis – He won four gold medals at the 1984 Olympics.

20. c) Chelsie Memmel – She returned to competition and helped the U.S. win team silver in 2008.

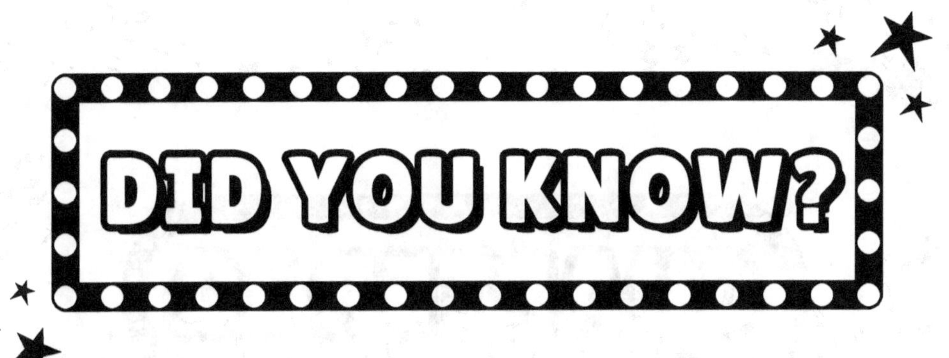

The first modern Olympic Games were held in Athens in 1896, with 241 athletes from 14 different nations competing in 43 events. The Olympics have since become the world's largest international sporting event, held every four years and watched by billions of people worldwide. The Games have evolved dramatically over the past 130 years, reflecting changes in society, technology, and global politics, yet they remain a powerful symbol of human achievement and international cooperation.

Jesse Owens' four gold medals at the 1936 Berlin Olympics became one of the most iconic moments in sports history, particularly because he achieved this feat in Nazi Germany, directly contradicting the regime's ideology of racial superiority. His performance demonstrated the power of sports to transcend politics and prejudice, inspiring generations of athletes and becoming a symbol of resistance against discrimination.

Women's participation in sports has grown exponentially since the early days of the Olympics. Charlotte Cooper of the United Kingdom became the first woman to win an Olympic gold medal in 1900 when she won the tennis competition. Today, women comprise nearly half of all Olympic competitors, a dramatic shift from the male-dominated early years of the Games. This evolution reflects broader social changes in gender equality and women's empowerment.

CHAPTER 10

The Ultimate Pop Culture Showdown

Pop culture brings generations together. Certain songs, TV moments, movie premieres, and live broadcasts become instant talking points, remembered long after the headlines fade. These are the moments people quoted, debated, and experienced in real time. From unforgettable performances to major events watched by millions, pop culture has shaped the soundtrack of the last seventy years. This chapter blends decades into one fast-moving challenge, testing how well you remember the moments that filled screens, speakers, and conversations.

1. Which television show first introduced the character Fonzie in the 1970s?

a. Laverne & Shirley
b. The Brady Bunch
c. Happy Days
d. Three's Company

2. Which 1982 song by Survivor became strongly associated with the film "Rocky III"?

a. Don't Stop Believin'
b. We Built This City
c. Another One Bites the Dust
d. Eye of the Tiger

3. Which toy craze swept playgrounds in the mid-1990s, featuring small plastic discs collected and traded by children?

a. Beanie Babies
b. Pogs
c. Tamagotchis
d. Furbies

4. In 1992, which late-night television moment stunned viewers when a singer ripped up a photo of the Pope live on air?

a. Madonna
b. Sinead O'Connor
c. Cher
d. Debbie Harry

5. In 1977, which singer's death shocked fans worldwide and was followed by massive public mourning at Graceland?

a. John Lennon
b. Jim Morrison
c. Elvis Presley
d. Freddie Mercury

6. Which 1984 pop star performed the hit song "Like a Virgin"?

a. Cyndi Lauper
b. Whitney Houston
c. Tina Turner
d. Madonna

7. In 1994, which figure skating scandal involving an attack on an Olympic rival dominated headlines?

a. Kristi Yamaguchi
b. Michelle Kwan
c. Tonya Harding
d. Katarina Witt

8. Which handheld game released in the late 1990s allowed players to raise a digital pet?

a. Game Boy
b. Furby
c. Tamagotchi
d. Skip-It

9. In 1998, which television series finale drew over 50 million viewers, making it one of the most watched episodes in U.S. history?

a. Seinfeld
b. Friends
c. ER
d. Frasier

10. Which 2009 song by Lady Gaga became one of the most streamed songs of the decade?

a. Born This Way
b. Poker Face
c. Just Dance
d. Bad Romance

11. In 1997, which funeral was watched by an estimated two billion people worldwide?

a. Queen Mother
b. Princess Margaret
c. Princess Diana
d. Grace Kelly

12. In 2004, which halftime show incident at the Super Bowl led to the phrase "wardrobe malfunction" becoming widely known?

a. Britney Spears
b. Christina Aguilera
c. Pink
d. Janet Jackson

13. In 2009, which pop icon's sudden death led to global tributes and record-breaking memorial viewership?

a. Prince
b. David Bowie
c. George Michael
d. Michael Jackson

14. In 1980, which former Beatle was tragically shot outside his New York City apartment building?

a. Paul McCartney
b. George Harrison
c. Ringo Starr
d. John Lennon

15. In 1999, which horror film became a surprise blockbuster after being marketed as "found footage"?

a. The Sixth Sense
b. The Haunting
c. The Faculty
d. The Blair Witch Project

16. In 2007, which celebrity's conservatorship became a major pop culture and legal story that continued into the 2010s?

a. Lindsay Lohan
b. Amanda Bynes
c. Britney Spears
d. Paris Hilton

17. Approximately how many people attended the Woodstock music festival in 1969?

a. About 50,000
b. About 250,000
c. About 400,000
d. About 1 million

18. In 1987, which television series finale became famous for revealing the entire season had been "a dream"?

a. Dynasty
b. Dallas
c. Cheers
d. Moonlighting

19. In 2011, which British singer's breakup album dominated charts worldwide?

a. Amy Winehouse
b. Duffy
c. Adele
d. Florence Welch

20. In 1968, which news anchor became a trusted national voice and was often called "the most trusted man in America"?

a. Tom Brokaw
b. Dan Rather
c. Peter Jennings
d. Walter Cronkite

1. c) Happy Days – Fonzie, played by Henry Winkler, became one of the most iconic characters of 1970s television.

2. d) Eye of the Tiger – Survivor's hit song became inseparable from Rocky III and defined early 1980s sports montages.

3. b) Pogs – These collectible plastic discs became a massive playground trading craze in the mid-1990s.

4. b) Sinead O'Connor – She shocked viewers in 1992 by tearing up a photo of the Pope live on Saturday Night Live.

5. c) Elvis Presley – His death in 1977 stunned fans worldwide and led to massive public mourning at Graceland.

6. d) Madonna – She performed "Like a Virgin," one of the defining pop hits of the 1980s.

7. c) Tonya Harding – The 1994 attack on rival Nancy Kerrigan became one of the most infamous sports scandals ever.

8. c) Tamagotchi – The handheld digital pet became wildly popular in the late 1990s.

9. a) Seinfeld – Its 1998 finale drew over 50 million viewers, making it one of the most watched episodes in U.S. history.

10. d) Bad Romance – Lady Gaga's hit became one of the most streamed and culturally dominant songs in 2009.

11. c) Princess Diana – Her 1997 funeral was watched by an estimated two billion people worldwide.

12. d) Janet Jackson – The 2004 Super Bowl halftime incident popularized the term "wardrobe malfunction."

13. d) Michael Jackson – His sudden death in 2009 triggered global tributes and record-breaking memorial viewership.

14. d) John Lennon – He was tragically shot outside his New York City apartment in 1980.

15. d) The Blair Witch Project – The 1999 horror film became a surprise blockbuster after being marketed as found-footage.

16. c) Britney Spears – Her conservatorship became a major pop culture and legal story spanning more than a decade.

17. c) About 400,000 – Although the festival was originally expected to draw far fewer, an estimated 400,000 people flooded the farm in upstate New York in August 1969, turning Woodstock into one of the largest and most iconic music gatherings in history.

18. b) Dallas – Its 1987 finale famously revealed that an entire season had been a dream.

19. c) Adele – Her 2011 album became one of the best-selling breakup records of the decade.

20. d) Walter Cronkite – He was widely referred to as "the most trusted man in America" during his tenure as a news anchor.

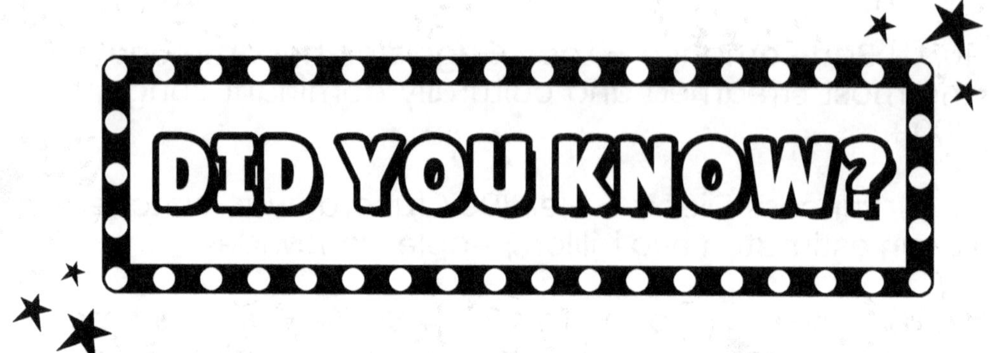

The Beatles' appearance on "The Ed Sullivan Show" on February 9, 1964, was watched by an estimated 73 million viewers, making it one of the most-watched television events in history. The performance launched the British Invasion and fundamentally changed American popular music and culture. Young people screamed so loudly during the performance that the band's music was barely audible, yet the cultural impact was undeniable and lasting.

Elvis Presley's influence on music and popular culture cannot be overstated. His unique blend of country, blues, and rock and roll, combined with his charismatic stage presence and controversial hip movements, made him a phenomenon. When he died in 1977, his death was mourned worldwide, and Graceland became a pilgrimage site for fans. Decades later, Elvis remains one of the most recognized and influential figures in entertainment history.

Michael Jackson's career spanned multiple decades and genres, but his peak came in the 1980s with the album "Thriller," which became the best-selling album of all time. His innovative music videos, particularly "Thriller" directed by John Landis, set new standards for the medium. When Jackson died in 2009, the global outpouring of grief demonstrated his universal appeal and the profound impact he had on music and popular culture worldwide.

Say What? Slang, Ads & Catchphrases

Every generation has its own words, slogans, and expressions that bring back a time and place. Some came from commercials, others from movies, music, or playground slang, and quickly became part of everyday life. A single line could define a decade or make a brand unforgettable. From iconic ads to once-trendy slang, these words helped shape culture. This chapter revisits the sayings and slogans that filled radios, televisions, and classrooms, and asks how many you still remember today.

1. Which company used the advertising slogan "Just do it"?

a. Reebok
b. Adidas
c. Nike
d. Puma

2. Which fast food chain was known for the slogan "Have it your way"?

a. McDonald's
b. Wendy's
c. Burger King
d. Taco Bell

3. The phrase "Where's the beef?" became popular in the 1980s through commercials for which company?

a. Arby's
b. Wendy's
c. Burger King
d. Dairy Queen

4. The slang term "groovy" was most strongly associated with which decade?

a. 1950s
b. 1960s
c. 1970s
d. 1980s

5. Which soda brand used the slogan "The real thing"?

a. Pepsi
b. Dr Pepper
c. Coca-Cola
d. 7 Up

6. The catchphrase "You're fired" became widely associated with which television personality in the 2000s?

a. Simon Cowell
b. Gordon Ramsay
c. Donald Trump
d. Mark Cuban

7. In the 1990s, the slang word "phat" was commonly used to describe something that was:

a. Expensive
b. Loud
c. Cool
d. Large

8. Which cereal brand featured the slogan "They're grrreat!"?

a. Cheerios
b. Frosted Flakes
c. Rice Krispies
d. Corn Pops

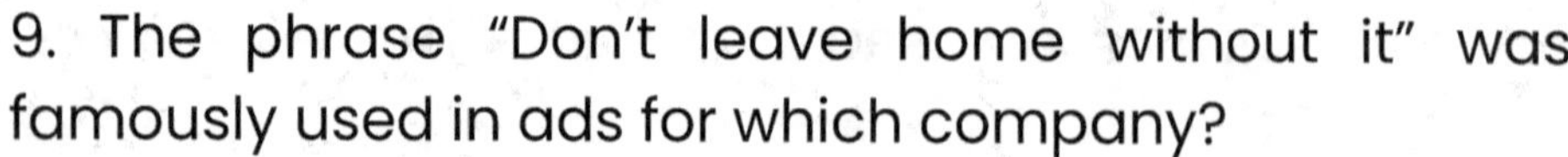

9. The phrase "Don't leave home without it" was famously used in ads for which company?

a. Visa
b. Mastercard
c. American Express
d. Discover

10. The 1970s catchphrase "Can you dig it?" generally meant:

a. Are you upset?
b. Do you understand?
c. Are you leaving?
d. Are you joking?

11. Which fast-food chain used the slogan "Have It Your Way"?

a. McDonald's
b. Burger King
c. Wendy's
d. Taco Bell

12. The phrase "You've come a long way, baby" was used in ads aimed at women for which product?

a. L'Oreal
b. Revlon
c. Clairol
d. Virginia Slims

13. Which gasoline company used the slogan "Put a tiger in your tank" during the 1960s?

a. Shell
b. Texaco
c. Esso
d. Mobil

14. Which laundry detergent brand used the slogan "Ring Around the Collar"?

a. Tide
b. Wisk
c. All
d. Cheer

15. Which reality television show popularized the phrase "The tribe has spoken"?

a. Big Brother
b. The Amazing Race
c. Survivor
d. The Bachelor

16. Which deodorant brand used the memorable slogan "Raise your hand if you're sure"?

a. Old Spice
b. Sure
c. Right Guard
d. Brut

17. The phrase "Sock it to me!" became popular on which late 1960s comedy show?

a. The Ed Sullivan Show
b. The Carol Burnett Show
c. Rowan & Martin's Laugh-In
d. The Smothers Brothers Comedy Hour

18. Which 1970s snack product advertised with the line "Bet you can't eat just one"?

a. Doritos
b. Pringles
c. Lay's Potato Chips
d. Fritos

19. The slang word "square" in the 1960s was used to describe someone who was:

a. Wealthy
b. Old-fashioned or uncool
c. Athletic
d. Honest

20. Which car rental company used the bold 1960s slogan "We try harder"?

a. Hertz
b. Avis
c. Budget
d. National

CHAPTER 11 ANSWERS

1. c) Nike – "Just do it" became one of the most recognizable advertising slogans in the world after launching in 1988.

2. c) Burger King – "Have it your way" emphasized customization and became a defining fast food slogan.

3. b) Wendy's – "Where's the beef?" became a national catchphrase in the 1980s.

4. b) 1960s – "Groovy" became a defining slang term of the counterculture era.

5. c) Coca-Cola – "The real thing" reinforced Coke's identity as the original cola.

6. c) Donald Trump – He made "You're fired" famous on the reality show "The Apprentice."

7. c) Cool – In the 1990s, "phat" meant impressive, stylish, or excellent.

8. b) Frosted Flakes – Tony the Tiger made "They're grrreat!" unforgettable.

9. c) American Express – "Don't leave home without it" became a powerful credit card slogan.

10. b) Do you understand? – "Can you dig it?" meant agreement or understanding in the 1970s.

11. b) Burger King - "Have It Your Way" became one of the most iconic fast-food slogans of all time, emphasizing customization and customer choice.

12. d) Virginia Slims – "You've come a long way, baby" targeted women during the 1960s and 70s.

13. c) Esso – "Put a tiger in your tank" was a memorable gasoline slogan of the 1960s.

14. b) Wisk - "Ring Around the Collar" was one of the most memorable and repetitive advertising jingles of the 1970s and 1980s.

15. c) Survivor – "The tribe has spoken" became one of reality television's most famous lines.

16. b) Sure – "Raise your hand if you're sure" made the deodorant brand instantly recognizable.

17. c) Rowan & Martin's Laugh-In – "Sock it to me!" became a signature catchphrase of the show.

18. c) Lay's Potato Chips – "Bet you can't eat just one" became one of the most memorable snack slogans.

19. b) Old-fashioned or uncool – In the 1960s, a "square" was someone seen as conventional or out of touch.

20. b) Avis – "We try harder" helped position Avis as a determined challenger brand in the 1960s.

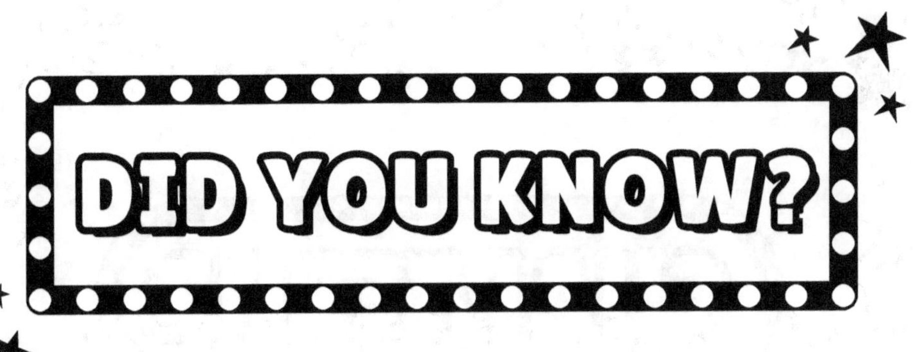

The term "slang" was defined by lexicographer Francis Grose in 1785, who described it as "cant" or "vulgar" language. However, slang has roots going back much further, with thieves' cant in 17th-century London being among the earliest documented forms. Slang has always served as a way for groups to creates a sense of identity and belonging.

Some of the most memorable advertising slogans have become so embedded in popular culture that people use them in everyday conversation without even thinking about their origins. Nike's "Just Do It" (1988), American Express's "Don't Leave Home Without It" (1975), and the California Milk Processor Board's "Got Milk?" (1993) are among the most influential advertising slogans of all time. These slogans succeeded because they were simple, memorable, and aligned perfectly with the values and aspirations of their target audiences.

The "Mean Joe Greene" Coca-Cola commercial from 1979 is considered one of the greatest TV commercials ever made. In the ad, a tough football player softens when offered a Coke, creating an emotional connection between the product and feelings of warmth and humanity. This commercial demonstrated that advertising could be art, telling a compelling story in just 60 seconds and creating a cultural moment that people still remember and reference decades later.

CHAPTER 12

Then & Now: Guess the Price & Before or After

Time has a funny way of playing tricks on memory. Some moments feel like they happened yesterday, while others seem much farther back than they really were. And when it comes to prices, what once felt expensive can now seem almost unbelievable. In this chapter, you will test your sense of time in two different ways. First, can you remember what everyday items actually cost? From groceries and gas to homes and entertainment, see if you can guess the real price from years past. Then comes the timeline challenge. Did it happen before or after 1975? Trust your instincts and see how sharp your memory really is.

1. In 1975, approximately how much did a loaf of bread cost in the United States?

a. About $0.25
b. About $0.50
c. About $0.85
d. About $1.20

2. In 1985, about how much did a brand new Ford Mustang cost?

a. About $7,500
b. About $10,000
c. About $14,000
d. About $18,000

3. Around 1968, what was the average monthly rent for an apartment in the United States?

a. About $60
b. About $120
c. About $250
d. About $400

4. In 1995, roughly how much did a gallon of milk cost?

a. About $1.10
b. About $1.80
c. About $2.50
d. About $3.75

5. In 1980, approximately how much did a brand new VCR cost?

a. About $150
b. About $300
c. About $600
d. About $1,000

6. In 1970, what was the average price of a movie ticket?

a. About $0.75
b. About $1.55
c. About $2.75
d. About $4.00

7. Around 1990, how much did a basic home computer typically cost?

a. About $400
b. About $800
c. About $1,500
d. About $2,500

8. In 1965, approximately how much did a dozen eggs cost?

a. About $0.35
b. About $0.62
c. About $1.10
d. About $1.75

9. In 1988, about how much did a Super Bowl ticket cost on average?

a. About $50
b. About $100
c. About $250
d. About $600

10. Around 2000, what was the average price of a new home in the United States?

a. About $120,000
b. About $170,000
c. About $240,000
d. About $325,000

11. The first episode of "Saturday Night Live" aired before or after 1975?

a. After
b. Before

12. The assassination of President John F. Kennedy happened before or after 1975?

a. After
b. Before

13. The release of the original "Jaws" movie happened before or after 1975?

a. After
b. Before

14. The Watergate scandal led to President Nixon's resignation before or after 1975?

a. After
b. Before

15. The launch of the Sony Walkman happened before or after 1975?

a. Before
b. After

16. The first Super Bowl was played before or after 1975?

a. Before
b. After

17. The fall of the Berlin Wall happened before or after 1975?

a. Before
b. After

18. The debut of "The Mary Tyler Moore Show" happened before or after 1975?

a. Before
b. After

19. The Challenger space shuttle disaster occurred before or after 1975?

a. Before
b. After

20. The opening of Walt Disney World in Florida happened before or after 1975?

a. Before
b. After

CHAPTER 12 ANSWERS

1. b) About $0.50 – In 1975, a loaf of bread typically cost around fifty cents, a price that now feels almost impossible.

2. b) About $10,000 – A brand new 1985 Ford Mustang was roughly ten thousand dollars, depending on the model and options.

3. b) About $120 – In the late 1960s, average monthly rent hovered a little over one hundred dollars in many parts of the country.

4. c) About $2.50 – By 1995, a gallon of milk commonly cost around two and a half dollars.

5. d) About $1,000 – Early VCRs were expensive luxury items, often priced near one thousand dollars in 1980.

6. b) About $1.55 – In 1970, the average movie ticket cost just over a dollar and a half.

7. c) About $1,500 – Around 1990, a basic home computer often cost well over a thousand dollars.

8. b) About $0.62 – In 1965, a dozen eggs typically sold for just over sixty cents.

9. b) About $100 – The average Super Bowl ticket in 1988 cost roughly one hundred dollars.

10. b) About $170,000 – Around the year 2000, the average new home price in the United States was about one hundred seventy thousand dollars.

11. a) After – The first episode of "Saturday Night Live" premiered in October 1975.

12. a) Before – President John F. Kennedy was assassinated in 1963.

13. b) After – The original "Jaws" was released in 1975.

14. a) Before – President Nixon resigned in 1974 as a result of the Watergate scandal.

15. b) After – The Sony Walkman was introduced in 1979.

16. a) Before – The first Super Bowl was played in January 1967.

17. b) After – The Berlin Wall fell in 1989.

18. a) Before – "The Mary Tyler Moore Show" debuted in 1970.

19. b) After – The Challenger disaster occurred in 1986.

20. a) Before – Walt Disney World opened in Florida in 1971.

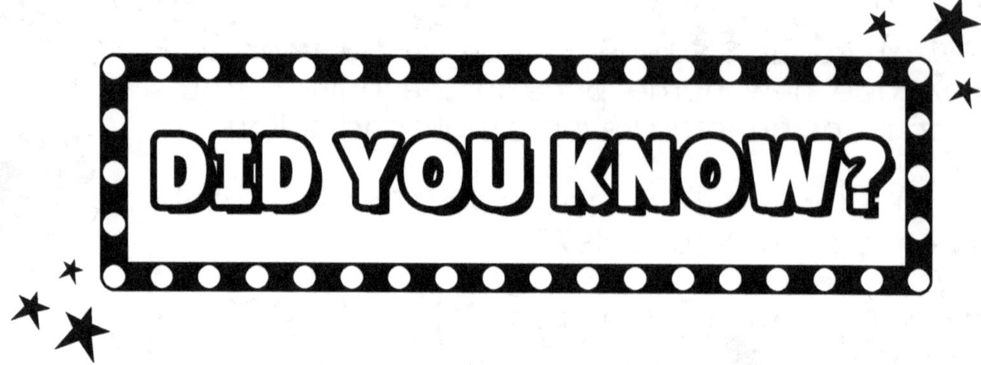

In the 1950s, the cost of living was dramatically different from today. A loaf of bread cost about 16 cents, a gallon of milk was around 90 cents, and ground beef was approximately 50 cents per pound. A $10 purchase could easily fill a shopping cart with groceries.

The price of gasoline in 1960 was approximately 31 cents per gallon, a figure that seems almost unbelievably cheap by today's standards. However, when adjusted for inflation, that 31 cents in 1960 would be equivalent to roughly $3.50 in 2026 dollars.

Housing prices have experienced some of the most dramatic increases over the past 70 years. In the 1950s, the median home price in America was around $8,000 to $10,000, while today the median home price exceeds $400,000 in many markets. This represents a far greater increase than general inflation, reflecting increased demand, limited housing supply, and changing preferences for larger homes with more amenities. These price changes reflect not just inflation but also fundamental shifts in the economy and society.

Some of the most important moments in the last seventy years weren't headlines. They were personal milestones. Take a few minutes to write down your memories. You might be surprised how much comes back.

Your First Car

What was it? What color was it? Did it have a name? Where did you drive first?

____

____

____

Your First Job

How old were you? What did you earn per hour? What did you spend your first paycheck on?

____

____

____

Your First Concert

Who did you see? Where was it? Do you remember
the ticket price? Was it as loud as you expected?

Your First Home

Was it an apartment, a house, or something else?
What did it cost? What do you remember most
about it?

The Biggest World Event You Remember

Where were you when it happened? Who were you
with? How did it make you feel at the time?

The Best Invention During Your Lifetime

What invention changed daily life the most?
Television? The internet? Smartphones? Something
else? Why do you think it mattered?

____

____

____

The Worst Fashion Trend You Survived

Platform shoes? Bell bottoms? Big hair? What did
you wear that you would never wear again?

____

____

____

Your Teenage Weekend Routine

What did a typical weekend look like for you as a
teenager? Who were you with, and what did you
usually do?

____

____

____

A Letter to My Family

If someone reads this book 20 years from now, what would you want them to know about your life?

____

____

____

____

____

____

____

____

____

____

CONCLUSION

Seventy years is more than just a number. It is a front-row seat to change, innovation, celebration, and challenge. You have watched the world move from black-and-white televisions to streaming screens in every pocket. You have seen music evolve from vinyl records to digital playlists, communication shift from handwritten letters to instant messages, and history unfold in real time. Through it all, everyday life kept moving, with its routines, traditions, and shared experiences.

This book has taken you through childhood memories, teenage milestones, cultural revolutions, unforgettable headlines, and the words and slogans that defined entire eras. Some answers may have come easily. Others may have sparked debate and laughter. What matters most is the journey through the moments that shaped a lifetime.

Seventy years means you have not just witnessed history. You have lived it.

Thanks for Reading!

Thanks for picking up this book! As a special thank-you, I've lined up some awesome freebies for you:

- *500 World War I & II Facts* — Digital edition
- *101 Idioms and Phrases* — Digital edition
- *1144 Random Facts* — Full audiobook

Scan the QR code below, enter your email, and all three bonuses will be on their way. Enjoy your extra content!

9 781923 722149